CAREERS IN
FASHION

Noel Chapman

fifth edition

**KOGAN
PAGE**

First published in 1984, written by Carole Chester
Second edition 1989
Third edition 1994, written by Noel Chapman
Fourth edition 1996
Fifth edition 1999

Kogan Page Limited
120 Pentonville Road
London N1 9JN   8 · 99

British Library Cataloguing in Publication Data

A CIP record for this book is available from the British Library.

ISBN 0 7494 2763 9

Typeset by Jean Cussons Typesetting, Diss, Norfolk
Printed and bound by Clays Ltd, St Ives plc

Contents

Introduction

Every edition of this book is different from, and, dare I say, better than, its predecessor. This, the fifth edition, is no exception – it's more up to date and in a new format; it's shorter, punchier but no less informative.

In response to changes and developments in fashion, education of fashion students is constantly providing new and updated courses to fulfil the industry's needs for graduates with an ever greater variety of skills and specialisms.

Fashion is a beguiling phenomenon – the driving force behind more and more areas of commerce, yet also its victim. Fashion is the breath of fresh air that brings change, variety and newness, as, from diverse and often exclusive beginnings new trends and ideas are discovered, fêted and exploited by its dependent industries. It becomes accessible, then, shortly after, commonplace, only to be superseded by the next breath, the next wave that makes everything in its wake look stale, old-fashioned, old hat!

As we look forward to the new millennium, fashion can clarify our position now, give us clues to the direction in which we are headed and a glimpse of the future.

If fashion is the thing that really excites you, if it looks like a world where you could really belong, then maybe a career in fashion is right for you. Maybe you have already decided that fashion is your future, but which aspect? What opportunities are there? You may have come to this book thinking that fashion is purely about designing clothes, yet there is so much more... there are dozens of related professions concerned with production, marketing, selling and promoting fashion.

Even when you are sure of your career choice, the routes you can take to make it a reality are not always clear. Where do you start? How long is the training? What qualifications do you need to have? What opportunities are open to you? These are just some of the questions that pose themselves and that this book aims to answer.

Are you going to be one of the first wave of graduates in the new millennium, do you see it as a chance to use your creativity and ideas – put your own spin on the world and how it will look over the next few decades? Yes? Then read on... .

1 About fashion and the fashion industry

The fashion cycle

The most exclusive area of the fashion industry is *haute couture* (high fashion), which is dominated by Paris and a few highly successful individuals or, rather, individual names. Many of them no longer exist as designers – the name and fashion house being kept alive by another designer. For example, Alexander McQueen at Givenchy works with a team of designers and assistant designers. In recent years, this trend of revitalizing older, established fashion 'house' names by introducing new design talent has resulted in many labels, such as Hermès, Gucci and Dior becoming hip and desirable again.

In almost all cases, the *haute couture* line – which is when clothes are individually designed and maybe a maximum of six of each piece are made to measure specifically for individual customers worldwide, at a cost of upwards of £5,000 per piece – does not make a profit. It is subsidized either by one or a number of cheaper lines, such as ready-to-wear, sportswear, diffusion, accessories, or by a house perfume.

In the case of Chanel – a fashion house that was revived by Karl Lagerfeld in the 1980s – the perfumes make more money than all the other lines put together. This is probably true of many of the older houses – certainly perfume is a huge money-spinner.

The newer designers make most of their money by licensing their names to other producers to make diffusion lines. These are simpler styles in less costly fabrics, made in larger quantities, that therefore cost less overall to make and can sell at a fraction of the cost of the main line. The big name designers also have deals with manufacturing companies to produce alternative lines for them. However, it is the main lines that are the most innovative and, therefore, influential in fashion terms – 'directional' is the word most often used for this effect.

Clearly, the designer cannot produce all the ideas for so many lines alone; there are teams of designers for each range, each line. The designer whose name is on the label may select from sketches the items to be sampled or may entrust selection to an assistant or assistants, only casting an eye over the final range.

Main ranges are produced twice yearly – shown in spring for the following winter, and autumn for the following spring/summer. In addition to this, there may be swimwear, seasonal sportswear (maybe skiwear) and a line christened by Americans 'cruise'. Cruise is a smaller range shown in high summer to be sold from December to February for winter holidays in the sun.

Lines are shown six months in advance of the retail season to give manufacturers time to produce the garments. Six months before the shows (that is, a year in advance of the season), the designers choose the fabrics and yarns. This time-scale gives the fabric and yarn companies time to produce samples and designers time to produce the sample garments for showing. The colour promoters show colour ideas a year to 18 months in advance of the designers choosing fabrics and yarns to enable the manufacturers to produce fabric in time for designers to sample. There is method in this apparent madness!

Those designers producing *haute couture* lines show them approximately six weeks before the main line. These shows are quieter affairs than those for the main lines and are presented in a salon-type environment to private customers and select members of the press. They often give the world its first glimpse of major fashion changes and offer designers a chance to test the water for responses to a new idea.

The showing of the main line - the *prêt-à-porter* (ready-to-wear) – is the big event that hits the headlines of the world's press. It is here that we see the major fashion events, the real media circuses. These shows often take place in specially erected marquees or hotel banqueting suites. More recently – in the frantic search for originality and novelty – other venues have included old theatres, a cattle market on the outskirts of Paris (some unfortunate parallels were drawn here!) and a back-street Paris parking lot, specially closed off for the event. Street fashion going full circle, you might say.

It is at these events – for this is really what they often are – that designers show their most extreme ideas, ones that are often overdone, overblown and overstyled, paraded on models, celebrity models and supermodels in an effort to project their names and images into the minds of the press and the buyers. There are no private individuals present at these special events, apart from a few celebrity guests to add further glitter and glamour. Many of the clothes are never intended to sell or be worn, created only to sell the idea – the thinking behind the collection.

There is often another whole range made to show buyers in the showroom. This selling often begins before the actual show! What appear in the shops six months later are toned- and pared-down versions of the creations that hit the runways, and headlines.

The largest section of the fashion market is actually the mass market – the wholesale manufacturers. Like the big name designers, they, too, often have their own, or house, style that their designers have to reflect in the ranges they come up with. Their role is to supply the high street shops, and ultimately the public, with affordable, wearable interpretations of the latest fashion styles.

The international fashion industry

There are but half a dozen capitals in the world of international fashion. The most important is still Paris, despite many attempts by other countries to supersede it; they steal the limelight for a season or two, but Paris counters with its unique flair.

This is not to say that other countries are not important, far from it. Based in Milan, the Italian fashion industry is enormous and balances its stylish ideas and inherent good taste with sound industrial backing. Japanese fashion is intellectually based and highly innovative, although the significant designers all show in Paris. However, fabrics and garments are nearly all produced in Japan.

The US fashion industry is based in New York and while its designers are rarely innovative, they have a particular knack of understanding contemporary customers' needs and rework the classics accordingly. Simple, modern, wearable clothes are their trademark and reflect the busy, cosmopolitan lives of New York's inhabitants.

Germany may not be able to boast as many celebrity designers as France or Italy, but the German fashion industry, founded on a long-established textile industry, is enormously significant, with one of the most high-tech fashion industries in Europe. Although more often associated with Paris, where she actually shows, the internationally renowned designer Jil Sander, hailed for her luxurious yet minimalist modern clothes, is actually based in Hamburg and runs her style empire from there.

The Spanish fashion industry, which declined in the 1950s and 1960s after the death of its premier couturier, Cristobal Balenciaga, is re-establishing itself. However, it is still viewed as the newcomer to the international scene and part of the whole cultural rebirth of Spain. Based in Barcelona, the Catalan capital, the Spanish can boast some highly innovative, creative and influential designers, but, as yet, the industry is comparatively small. The longer-established textile industry is internationally renowned, however, and supports and promotes its designers in the manner of the Italians.

London is doubtless Britain's fashion centre as far as trends and new ideas are concerned, with most of the manufacturing being done in the Midlands and north of England, close to the textile industries.

While Britain, by virtue of its unrivalled art education system, produces some of the world's most creative designers, the fashion industry still does not, unfortunately, have the kind

of backing from government and industry that its global coun-
terparts enjoy. It has to make do with less satisfactory venues,
ones that are often cramped and unsuitable. Poor organization
and underfunding means that many designers simply cannot
match their European competitors' standards. The press, in an
effort to compensate and ever determined to assert London as
the world's creative fashion capital, often choose a little-known
and ill-prepared designer to catapult into the season's limelight
as the next big thing; 'the new Galliano', 'the next McQueen'
are favourite expressions of Britain's press. Sadly, without
strong financial backing and a well-trained support team, many
of these designers, talented though they may be, enjoy only
momentary celebrity before their businesses fail and they join
the ranks of hundreds of others who also fell foul of the power
of the press and disinterest of government and industry.

In order to fulfil their ambitions, many designers go abroad
to work. Many of the world's biggest fashion companies send
talent scouts to the college degree shows to headhunt new
talent. It is common to find that the key designers behind the
world's big names are British-trained or that the finance behind
many of Britain's designer labels is, in fact, overseas money. In
the last couple of years, there has, however, been a slow trend
for backing in this country. A few of the more entrepreneurial
high street chains and one of the big department stores,
Debenhams, are building small portfolios of designers with
whom they produce small collections at more affordable prices
than their designers' main lines. Marks & Spencer often works
in a similar way, employing designers to develop small ranges –
unfortunately, usually marketed anonymously or as consultants
and advisers for particular clothing areas.

That is a brief summary of the world's fashion centres, but
the picture would be incomplete without a mention of the
great fashion production centres. While Britain, France,
Germany, Italy and the United States all have significant home-
based fashion production industries, all depend heavily on
economical, quality, high-volume production companies in the
Middle and Far East – particularly Hong Kong, which, over
the years, has developed some of the world's most advanced
production units. With the changes in the political climate over

the past few years, we are beginning to see northern Europe develop its industrial potential and European fashion companies are starting to initiate production closer to home.

How can you find out more about fashion?

If you're interested in fashion but feel you don't know that much about it, it is easy enough to brush up your knowledge. While we criticize it, *The Clothes Show* on television fulfils its aims quite successfully and does give some information and insight, particularly when covering the international fashion shows. As yet, this is the only British TV programme to attempt serious coverage of fashion issues. Those lucky enough to have Sky TV can see a number of late-night fashion programmes, although these all have a strong US slant.

More and more designers and design-led companies have Web sites and those of you with a little time and a few detective skills can soon tap into a rapidly expanding resource of up-to-the-minute fashion information.

Your local library should have a reasonable selection of books on the subject and its periodicals section can provide you with an up-to-date fashion picture. Many of the best fashion magazines that cover the fashion seasons in depth (*Collezioni, Fashion Line, Moda Book, International Fashion Trends, Men's Collection* and so on) are usually prohibitively expensive, even for libraries (given their limited readership). However, large stationers often have an excellent range and there is no charge for browsing – the worst they can do is ask you to move on if you're not going to buy! Many magazines now also have pages on the Internet.

Once you have started on a course and found a lecturer to sponsor you, you may apply for a ticket to use the library at the Victoria and Albert Museum or the British Library. Two other costume libraries that students enter by appointment are at the Fashion Research Centre in Bath and the Gallery of English Costume in Manchester. There are, however, more than 120 museums and galleries in the UK that have costume collections. *Museums and Galleries in Great Britain and Northern Ireland,* published annually, gives a short entry for each museum arranged by county – your local library should hold a copy of this.

Another way to find out about contemporary fashion is simply to look around the shops. If you've been looking at magazines, you'll know that the back pages list shops where you can see the merchandise featured. Most largish towns have at least one shop selling 'designer clothes' and the high street chains are often very good at reflecting what's happening. If you are going on a research browse, it may be a good idea not to go on their busiest day (often Saturday). When you go, chat to the sales staff and tell them why you are looking. They are often more than pleased to talk you through their ranges. Lastly, there is no substitute for actually looking at real people and real clothes to get your 'eye in' (see also Chapter 8, Further Reading).

2 Deciding on fashion

Where do your interests lie?

Maybe you know exactly what you want to do – maybe you even know the route you want to take to achieve it – but are you aware of all the opportunities, all the routes and all the courses available? For example, you may want to do a fashion degree course – especially if you have the GCSEs and A levels required – but that isn't the only option, or indeed the only route, to take if you want to get a degree.

Many people begin with a general interest in art and design, with experience of only one or two areas, and would like the opportunity to try other areas before committing themselves to a specialism. Alternatively, perhaps, like myself and many others who became involved in fashion via the art foundation route, you believe as fashion takes its inspirations from, and goes hand-in-hand with, so many subjects, not least art and design, a good, broad grounding in these areas can only be beneficial.

In young people there is often a natural interest in fashion, but deciding whether or not this is the career option for you can often take time and some experience of the other art/design areas.

Is training really necessary?

Entering the art and design field inevitably means spending between two and five years (or more if you go on to complete a postgraduate course) in higher education. Few people manage to succeed as practising artists or designers without having an art and design education, and natural talent and interest are not the only considerations.

Art and design education in Britain has developed over the years to provide the creative, theoretical, technical and personal elements that equip its graduates with the basics skills and attitudes they need to begin their careers. Often it is not until near completion of their courses that many people actually become aware of exactly where their true interests and abilities lie, when, indeed, the full range of career opportunities opens up to them and what they require becomes apparent.

Alternatively, if you are not creative and know for sure that this is not the route for you, if you want to work among creative people, perhaps on the administration side, for a fashion company, if you have the right personality and personal skills, maybe a course involving secretarial and computer skills would provide you with the right background to work in such an area. In all types of employment there is a critical shortage of trained people with advanced IT skills – rumours are flying around that many employers and recruitment bureaux are actually searching abroad for trained staff. With this in mind, training that includes a sound grounding in computer skills can only be of benefit to anyone expecting to be in the job market in a few years' time. Similarly, while you don't particularly need qualifications to be, say, a model, if you want to be involved in fashion as a booker, perhaps, then you need good secretarial and interpersonal skills. The competitive nature of the world of work makes the possession of recognized qualifications increasingly important in all fields.

What kind of course would suit you?

You can find out more about subject choices and courses at all levels in Chapter 3, Studying Fashion. What really matters for your choice of course is very much determined by your personal interests and qualities (qualifications are a factor here, too, but we shall discuss these in Chapter 3 also).

So, you're interested in fashion, but do you want to be a designer? Are you interested in making things, in perfecting a product maybe, or are you actually more interested in the textile or fabric side? Do you like selling? Perhaps you'd like to go into retail and be a buyer or merchandiser. Public relations (PR) is promoting – like selling, but in a different way. Perhaps you'd be selling the designer or the idea or concept, maybe to the press or public rather than a product as such. Are you very aware and clued-up? Would you like to do forecasting and trend work? Maybe you are smitten by magazines and would like to create the fashion stories and images using clothes from other designers and retailers – perhaps you see yourself as a stylist?

Certain qualities are important factors in your decision about which area of fashion to go for. How do you work in a team? Are you happier working on your own? Do you mind being told what to do? Can you organize people/things? Can you negotiate or be diplomatic? The list is endless, but try discussing these points with other people – professional as well as social.

Answering a few of these kinds of questions as best you can may help you decide on the type of career that would suit you best.

The next step is to ask 'What sort of course do I want/need to do?'

An academic course

An academic course, such as history of fashion, is one on which you may explore the academic study of the history and appreciation of fashion and costume without necessarily being involved in the practice.

A design course

These can vary in their focus. Some put the accent on creativity and innovation, but there are a few such courses where the bias towards creativity over practicality is so strong that it's closer to fine art and performance art. Other design courses focus more on commercialism and practicality.

A styling, communication and promotion course

Maybe you don't see yourself as a designer, but would like to be involved with magazines and PR instead. This is the kind of course for you.

A manufacturing course

You're much more interested in the construction and production of clothes than the design or retail aspects. Such a course will focus on these aspects of fashion.

A fashion and textile course

You're interested in textiles, the unique links between fabric and the body, the textural and tactile elements of fashion. A course of this kind is more open in this way.

A fashion and textile technology course

If you're quite scientific and interested in practical elements rather than being artistic and creative, this could be the direction for you.

An illustration course

Fashion illustration does not usually appear as a whole subject in itself – it is more common for it to be an option, sometimes as part of a communication and promotion course. Nearly always it will be linked with some garment construction. As most successful illustrators will verify, they started off doing designing courses. The general thinking is that the best illustrators are the ones who understand how garments are constructed and work.

A specialist course

There are some courses that concentrate on the practice and study of specialized aspects of fashion in depth. Courses exist for footwear, corsetry, knitwear, sportswear, millinery and so on, while many courses that don't have a specialism as such have a distant flavour or bias because of their links with industry and professional contacts, location and so on.

A fashion photography course

Unfortunately, there is little choice in terms of courses that actually specialize in fashion photography, although a number do lean in this direction. Most professional photographers start off learning all aspects of photography and then specialize in fashion later on. Many fashion courses include some photography, but mainly as a supporting study. Some communication and promotion courses have a strong leaning towards photography, often with video.

Courses for non-creative areas

Courses exist at all levels in secretarial, business and management studies, though most are quite general and so you may have to make your own connections to get into the fashion industry in particular.

Points to bear in mind

Many degree courses offer the option of a European language (with some it is seen as an integral part of the course and therefore compulsory).

Most courses these days include business and professional studies; some include fashion marketing. How much will vary and, as with academic content, read the prospectus to find out the balance and weighting of a particular course.

Remember that courses come as a package – even though there may be options, you can't just pick the bits you wish and leave out the rest. There has to be some academic and professional study in order that the course has the right 'weight' to merit the status of a qualification. So, it's worth reading the prospectus and the student handbook properly and asking the right questions at the college open day. Talk to staff and, as always, talk to students.

When do you have to decide on a specialism?

If you are taking the creative route into the fashion industry, you may begin with a foundation course. You will have to decide on your specialism at Christmas of the final year of a two-year course or, if it is a one-year one, again, at Christmas, but in that case at the end of the first term.

If you decide not to begin with a foundation course at an art and design college, you could take a BTEC two-year National Diploma in General Art and Design or a BTEC First Diploma (for those without formal entry qualifications). These courses offer the opportunity to test out areas you have not yet explored, as well as those that are familiar to you, such as graphics or textiles, and, importantly, to develop existing basic skills, such as drawing and use of colour, media and so on. However, especially on a one-year course, time is short. If you are preparing for entry to degree or vocational courses in the following year, you will need to decide your chief area of study at the end of the first term or early in the spring term so that there is time to prepare relevant work for your portfolio to take to interviews.

While completing this course, you should also, in your own time, be extending your knowledge of fashion by finding out everything you can about the industry – who the new and influential names are, not just the mega-names. College inter-viewers get awfully bored when applicants quote the obvious – Westwood or Versace or whoever – as their favourite designers, when it would show much more awareness to be able to discuss a newer, lesser-known name in the fashion world. Individual research and documentation is very helpful for self-development.

How motivated are you?

Are you following on with a subject that you are good at? 'Art is my best subject at school and I'm really interested in fashion, so it seems a natural move to pursue this at college.' How good are you really? Even if it is your best subject, you may not measure up to the standards expected at art school and beyond. Enjoying art and having an interest in fashion at school is one thing, but are you sufficiently devoted to follow it through for maybe three, four or even five years in higher education? Being able to draw to a reasonable standard is one skill, but being able to generate ideas on demand is quite another. Are you prepared to take on the academic and theoretical work involved? Why not seek your art teacher's opinion about your abilities as he or she should be able to give you some guidance as to the most suitable course for you.

Take a look at yourself

It will come as no surprise that, of all the careers in art and design, fashion is probably the most competitive. Courses to study fashion are very popular. When deciding, you must ask yourself if you have the right personal attributes for this demanding and exciting field. The following checklist may help.

Is fashion right for me?

A career in fashion is the perfect job for me because I:

❑ am passionate about clothes and fashion;
❑ am highly creative and ambitious;
❑ have an aptitude for visual expression – drawing, painting, cutting, making, exploring colour and texture;
❑ am interested in how clothes are made;
❑ have the ability to research information and communicate findings;

❏ have the determination to work projects through to achieve solutions;

❏ can work to deadlines on my own or as part of a team;

❏ have a facility for organizing and analysing material and making reasoned critical judgements;

❏ have a curiosity and interest in society and the environment;

❏ am fascinated by change and development.

If your answer to many of the above is 'Yes', you could be right to choose a career in fashion.

What if you are not brilliant at art, but do have a strong interest in one aspect or another of fashion? Maybe a more technical fashion course is right for you. It's worth finding out what is on offer in the way of courses and what a college is looking for in an applicant. If you have a part-time or Saturday job, maybe in retail, talk to your boss or other people within the company. Talk to anyone you know, or know of, who is connected with the industry.

It is sometimes possible to arrange an advisory interview at your local art or technical college where you can speak to a tutor and even show some of your work. Find out when the open days are at your local colleges and be sure to go. Write down a few questions to ask – it's odd how everyone's mind goes blank in these situations. During early summer, the degree or diploma shows are open to the public. These provide an opportunity to see the type and quality of work produced and a chance to talk to students about their work and education experiences.

For many people, choosing a career in any art and design subject may be seen as a soft option. Indeed, this may be a point you have to counter with people when announcing your decisions. Such courses are often mistakenly seen as less demanding than other academic degree courses. This would be a very negative reason for choosing the subject and lack of positive interest would be revealed at an interview. Any student or tutor will tell you that, whatever course you choose to follow, the demands made on you are considerable – creatively, technically and intellectually – particularly on degree courses. There are a few courses where you would be solely concerned with practical work and some more rigorous than others, but all have structures and timetables.

Most courses require a high degree of self-motivation on the part of students, who have to generate, organize and plan their own work. The apparent freedoms are a challenge in themselves. Technical and theoretical studies are vital to support a student's practical work. Assessments are regular, as they are for any kind of course, and may include exams and essays as well as discussions and assessment of your work with tutors and examiners. The expected intellectual and academic requirements are reflected in the courses' minimum entry requirements, which are similar to those of other subjects in higher education, many requiring GCSEs and A levels in academic subjects. Entry requirements for courses are explained in Chapter 3.

Job security

When choosing a course, remember that, whatever you study, there is no guarantee of a job at the end of it. The job market is always unpredictable and, in times of economic difficulty, fashion/clothes is one of the first areas people cut back on. This has a knock-on effect right through the industry.

Qualifications are not the only factors to be evaluated by employers when you enter the job market. Your skills and talents, general suitability for the job, personality, appearance and ability to fit in are all important. The geographical area in which you are looking and the general competitiveness of the job market are all going to feature in your search for a job. So, choosing a course for what it promises at the end may not turn out to be a wise decision. If you are concerned about your career prospects, read more about occupations and the careers of fashion design graduates in Chapter 4.

Personal satisfaction

As with all art and design subjects (although not a particularly prominent idea these days), not all students of fashion are concerned about their employment prospects. Rather, they see a design course as a way of exploring an area in depth and for their own personal development. Many tutors, students and ex-students will still say this is the best reason for wanting to do a course. This is because you then value the opportunity to spend some time exploring new freedoms, extending your creative and intellectual skills, acquiring knowledge of techniques, new skills, styles and approaches to your work and finding your own direction and expression through your artwork. Conversely, depending on the nature and individual flavour of the course you are applying for, being very focused and determined to aim for a particular job in a particular sector of the market and knowing your abilities and limitations may reflect a college's ideal student profile.

Who can you talk to about fashion?

Talking to other people about career plans is a good way of testing your motivation. Parents, teachers, friends and careers advisers may encourage you, direct you or dissuade you from choosing fashion design for a number of reasons:

◆ They may feel it is a waste of time.
◆ They may feel that fashion design does not lead to 'useful' or 'secure' jobs.
◆ They may feel that you don't have to go to college to 'make frocks'.
◆ They may try to persuade you to choose what they perceive as a more academic subject.
◆ They may feel that other areas of higher education and training would be more worthwhile or suit you better.

Be sure you are well enough informed to meet these challenges. If you can resist these pressures successfully, you will prove to yourself, and to others, that you are sufficiently motivated.

Here is a checklist of people who might be able to help:

- art, design and craft teachers at school; art and design tutors in art colleges;
- careers teachers, year tutors and careers advisers, who can help you to weigh up your abilities, interests and values, and then assist you in assessing fashion/art and design in relation to other subjects or occupational areas;
- parents, friends, relations and past students from your school or college who have been at art school and can tell you about their experiences;
- fashion/art and design students at your local college;
- if you have a Saturday or a part-time job in retail or a contact in a fashion-related area, people within the company.

3 Studying fashion

What qualifications will I need to study for?

It is likely that, if you want to be a fashion designer, you will need to study on a course at a higher education institution. There are various specialized courses on offer. It is important to look at the course content of both BTEC Higher National Diplomas (HNDs) and degrees. While in other subject areas an HND may be considered a lesser qualification than a degree, in art and design – and particularly fashion – the emphasis is as much on technical skills as creativity. As always, it is important to judge individual courses on their merits. However, it is also important for those intending to undertake a course in fashion (or any other branch of art and design) to note that no specific level of education is indispensable for, or guarantees, any particular type or level of job. In the fashion business, job titles and functions are not clear cut. People with different job titles and different levels of qualification may do the same job. Career progression in the industry is achieved on merit, through experience gained, as expressed in a portfolio of work.

This chapter describes the training and courses on offer in fashion and textiles. While at craft level it is possible to train on the job and study part time, to enter at the higher levels will almost certainly require some form of full-time training. This whole subject is made more complicated by the fact that courses with the same title and at the same level will not have the same emphasis or content. No two courses are the same. Thorough research will be required on your part.

Fashion, and fashion and textiles, courses exist at all levels of qualifications, either as specialist courses in themselves or as part of more general art and design courses. The study areas are characterized by two main types of course titles: 'fashion design' (encompassing womenswear, menswear, knitwear, footwear and accessory design), and 'textile design' (where the body and fabric are combined in a more experimental way).

Uniquely, fashion has creative, technical and business dimensions. These are reflected in the levels and range of courses available. At some levels, studies are likely to include general design, professional practice, techniques such as weaving, printing and dyeing, pattern cutting, sewing skills, machine and handknitted fabrics and clothing. At the higher levels, courses are likely to include business and management studies, covering marketing, accounts, commerce and economics. At HND and degree level, courses may have options in fashion promotion, retailing and journalism. Some courses have one-year industrial placements in the UK or abroad. Proficiency in a European language may then be a requirement.

There are also some courses dedicated to the study of a specialized area of fashion and design – for example, embroidery or footwear design.

Schools cannot always teach the range of art and design activities found in the outside professional world. They will, in the main, cover the core drawing, painting and craft skills. If you are considering higher education in fashion or any other specialized area, you should also look seriously at the courses on offer in colleges of further education. This chapter is concerned with outlining the courses available. To help you make the right first choice of course and gain a clear understanding of the progression from one course to the next, Table 3.1 – a summary of qualifications – and Figure 3.1 – ways in which to gain qualifications and related studies – provide a simplified but useful overview of the courses on offer and how they fit together. As the world of fashion is so vast and varied, it follows that the range of courses that may help you on your way to a career in fashion is vast and varied also. For reasons of practicality, not all of them can be listed here. For a full listing of all

Table 3.1 *Summary of qualifications*

Work-based qualification	NVQs CGLI (part time)	These qualifications are studied for while working and will normally qualify to craft level
Further education (vocational)	BTEC First/GNVQ Intermediate BTEC National/GNVQ Advanced C&G (full time)	The courses are designed for entry into employment. At the higher level they also qualify students for entry into higher education
Further education (academic)	Foundation courses A levels	These courses are designed as preparation for higher education. The foundation course is the preferred method of entry
Higher education	HNDs Degrees	HNDs and degrees offer very specific courses. It is important to research the content carefully
Postgraduate and advanced studies	Entry into specialist occupations Art Therapy Art Administration Teaching	At postgraduate level, you may wish to extend specialist art education or qualify for a specialist occupation
Professional qualifications	Chartered Society of of Designers (CSD) Royal Society of Arts (RSA) British Display Society (BDS) Associate of the Textile Institute (ATI) Licentiate of Society of Designer Craftsmen (LSDC)	These are particular to the area you wish to study to become a member of a professional body. They are most likely to be included as part of a vocational course
Mature students	Access Portfolio preparation	While mature students may use the traditional routes outlined above, Access courses have been specially designed to cater for the needs of adults returning to education. Portfolio preparation courses assist those with artwork to put it in order for HE applications

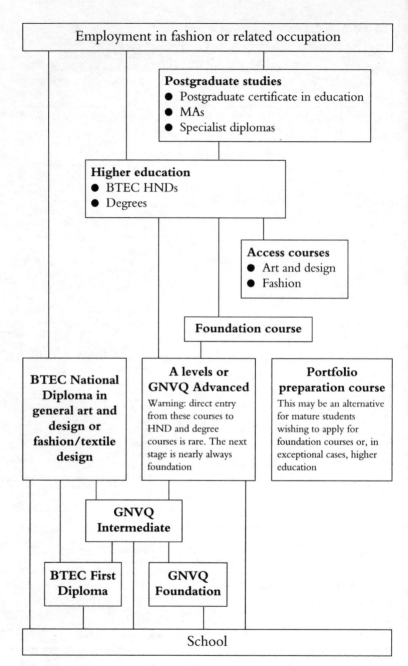

Figure 3.1 *Qualification routes in fashion and related studies*

the courses available, consult up-to-date course directories and reference books, most of which are available in local libraries. As new courses are validated constantly, you should always check with the most recently updated source of the relevant information. You may also contact the National Student Helpline, Learning Direct, on 0800 100900. Entry qualifications can vary from college to college. The UCAS Web site (see Chapter 7 for address) has an up-to-date list of courses and course descriptions.

There are several acronyms that you will encounter as you research your preferred route to a qualification in fashion. It is important to be clear exactly what they mean. Below you will find out not only what all those letters stand for but, more importantly, what kind of study is involved and the different levels there are for each type of qualification.

National Vocational Qualifications (NVQs)

The National Council for Vocational Qualifications (NVQs) has established a framework for vocational qualifications in defined occupational areas. These denote the level of qualification achieved as follows:

◆ *Level 1* (Basic): for jobs and occupations where requirements are limited;
◆ *Level 2* (Standard): for many common jobs and occupations;
◆ *Level 3* (Advanced): for skilled jobs and occupations;
◆ *Level 4* (Higher): for occupations with a specialist, supervisory or professional requirement;
◆ *Level 5* (Postgraduate).

NVQ qualifications recognize skills and knowledge gained on the job. Thus assessment of competences in the workplace is involved and the student is required to build up a portfolio of work proving that prescribed elements of these have been met. Students can progress at their own pace. The awarding bodies for these qualifications include Qualifications For Industry (QFI), which is part of the CAPITB, and City and Guilds. The scope and range of NVQs in the industry is increasing all the time. This qualification is offered by employers and the providers of youth training programmes.

General National Vocational Qualifications (GNVQs)

General National Vocational Qualifications (GNVQs) are relatively new. They cover broad occupational areas, such as art and design, business, health and social care, leisure and tourism, catering, built environment and information technology. They offer core skills as well as those for a particular occupational area. They are designed as an alternative to A level studies and may be run at schools and colleges. There are three levels of courses:

◆ *Foundation:* qualifies for entry to the intermediate course, usually taking one year;
◆ *Intermediate:* equivalent to four GCSEs, usually taking one year;
◆ *Advanced:* equivalent to at least two A levels, usually taking two years.

GNVQ Intermediate in art and design

This is a one-year course that can be taken as an alternative to GCSEs. There are no specialist areas to be covered. Progression is usually achieved by then going on to do a BTEC National or GNVQ Advanced course.

Entry requirements: no formal entry requirements.

GNVQ Advanced in general art and design

This is a two-year course. Four GCSEs and the presentation of a portfolio are required to get a place on this course. It may be taken as an alternative to A levels by school students. Progression is achieved by then going on to do a Higher

National Diploma or a degree. There are specialized National or GNVQ Advanced courses in fashion. Many BTEC National Diploma and HND courses are changing their designations to GNVQ Advanced courses.

Entry requirements: successful completion of BTEC First or GNVQ Intermediate or four GCSEs at C or above, plus presentation of a portfolio.

Business and Technology Education Council (BTEC) courses

The Business and Technology Education Council is a body that validates over 400 art and design courses at 135 colleges across the UK. The aim of the BTEC is to offer employment-related courses. In art and design, these are offered at three levels:

◆ BTEC First Diploma/Certificate;
◆ BTEC National Diploma/Certificate;
◆ BTEC Higher National Diploma/Certificate.

BTEC First Diploma in art and design

This is a one-year course that can be taken as an alternative to GCSEs. There are no specialist areas to be covered. Progression is usually achieved by then going on to do a BTEC National or GNVQ Advanced course.

Entry requirements: no formal entry requirements.

BTEC National Diploma in general art and design

This is a two-year course. Four GCSEs and the presentation of a portfolio are required to get a place on this course. It may be taken as an alternative to A levels by school students. Progression is achieved by then going on to do a Higher

National Diploma or a degree. There are specialized National or GNVQ Advanced courses in fashion. Many BTEC National Diploma and HND courses are changing their designations to GNVQ Advanced courses.

Entry requirements: successful completion of BTEC First or GNVQ Intermediate or four GCSEs at C or above, plus presentation of a portfolio.

BTEC Higher National Diploma in design (fashion/textiles)

These are vocationally specific courses. A wide range of courses is available with specialisms in fashion or fashion and textiles. Many offer options in business studies, fashion promotion, illustration, accessing designs and millinery. These courses normally involve two years' full-time study or three years' if an industrial placement is included in the course. The emphasis on these courses is technical.

The BTEC HND in business and finance may be taken with a specialism in fashion business at Croydon College or the London College of Fashion (part of the London Institute) or with fashion retail at the London College of Distributive Trades.

The BTEC HND in science (leather technology) may be taken at Nene College.

A Diploma of Higher Education in textile and fashion design is offered at the University of Ulster.

Entry requirements: minimum age 18 on 31 December of year of entry; BTEC or SCOTVEC National Diploma or Certificate; successful completion of a foundation course; Advanced GNVQ in art and design; Scottish Certificate of Education; an approved Access to Higher Education certificate.

General information

BTEC qualifications can be taken both in general art and design and in specialized areas, such as fashion and textiles, millinery, footwear and visual communication. Full-time courses are normally free to most students under 19 (under 18 in some areas).

In Scotland, the Scottish Vocational Education Council (SCOTVEC) offers two-year National and Higher National Diploma courses with equivalent entry requirements to those for BTEC courses.

As mentioned above, the BTEC National Diploma in general art and design is increasingly being redesignated as a GNVQ Advanced course. Note too that BTEC and the University of London Examination and Assessment Council have combined under the umbrella heading of the Edexcel Foundation (see Chapter 7 for contact details). BTEC forms the vocational division of Edexcel, but will continue to operate as usual for the present.

For students who wish to give themselves a broad creative base, a general art and design National Diploma may be a good choice, providing opportunities to explore a range of art and design areas, develop basic skills and go on to more specialist study at a higher level. The BTEC National Diploma may itself be taken in specialist areas. Here is a list of the courses that are most relevant to fashion:

◆ Fashion;
◆ Design (Fashion/Textiles);
◆ Design (Textiles);
◆ Design (Photography).

City and Guilds of London Institute (CGLI)

City and Guilds (C&G) is the largest technical testing and qualifying body in Britain. It produces schemes of technical education, sets examinations and establishes national standards of expertise. It is also an awarding body for NVQs. Courses leading to these qualifications are provided by schools, colleges and further education and training centres. Many are only available on a part-time or evening basis so that they can be taken up by those in employment to complement industrial training and experience. There are some full-time courses available. These are career qualifications that recognize the different standards of technical skill and knowledge needed within an occupation. The levels of study are:

◆ *Part 1:* Operative;
◆ *Part 2:* Craft Level;
◆ *Part 3:* Advanced Craft Level.

A number of full-time City and Guilds courses are offered at colleges in creative studies and clothing, footwear and leather goods. These courses are not widely available. Many have been integrated into other study programmes. The courses usually last two years to complete parts 1 and 2.

Entry requirements: no specific entry qualifications. There are several specific City and Guilds courses in fashion and related studies. These courses can be completed on either a full- or part-time basis. The course titles and City and Guilds numbers are as follows:

◆ *Creative Studies:* separate certificates are awarded for the following courses:
   – 780 Fashion;
   – 782 Embroidery;
   – 795 Textiles;
   – 796 Lacemaking;
   – 797 Machine Knitting.
◆ *Clothing, Footwear and Leather Goods:* the courses are:
   – 414 Textile Techniques;
   – 454 Footwear Manufacture (Stages 1 and 2);
   – 456 Leather Manufacture (Operatives);
   – 457 Leather Manufacture (Craft);
   – 460 Clothing Craft (Stages 1, 2 and 3);
   – 460–2 Certificate in Organizational and Supervisory Studies in the Garment Industry;
   – 461 (Special) Furriery;
   – 468 Knitting Machine Mechanics (Craft, Advanced Craft, Senior Craftsman Certificate);

- 469 Clothing machine mechanics (Craft, Advanced Craft);
- 470 Leather Goods Manufacture (Ordinary, Advanced);
- 475 Rural Saddlery;
- 498 Leather Manufacture, Dyeing and Finishing Techniques.

Foundation courses

All degree courses and some vocational courses require students to have completed a foundation course, although those with at least two A levels may be exempted by the college (in Scotland, foundation studies are included in full-time vocational and degree courses). Many students keep other options open by taking A levels prior to a foundation. There is usually a lot of competition to get on foundation courses. Some local education authorities will only fund those attending local courses.

Entry requirements: minimum age 17; five GCSEs at C grade or above; some colleges prefer at least one A level subject.

While A levels provide the main and traditional route into higher education for almost all other subject areas, this is not the case with art and design courses, where to gain entry with A levels is the exception. However, it is always possible where exceptional ability or experience can be demonstrated. This is known as direct entry. Some colleges will say that they do admit some students on the basis of A levels.

Many students do take A levels and then a foundation course. Most foundation courses will ask for students coming straight from school to have at least one A level. Students pursuing this route may consider business studies or a language as a useful additional A level to art, as success in the fashion industry may well rely on business acumen. Many of the higher-level courses have some business content for this reason.

Some degree courses are now offering four-year courses with the first year being an integral foundation year, counted as year zero of the degree. This means that eligible students receive a grant for their foundation year and are automatically accepted on to the degree after successful completion of this year zero study.

Foundation courses give broad grounding in all aspects of art and design. They provide students with the opportunity to work in a variety of materials. These include printing and textiles, but also sculpture, painting and three-dimensional design. These courses are often referred to as 'diagnosis courses'. They provide, as their name suggests, a chance for students to assess their abilities and test their commitment to particular areas of work. If you are interested in progressing on to a fashion course in higher education, then in this year you will be able to reflect that emphasis in the portfolio you produce.

Mature students' entry into higher education

For mature students, direct entry to art and design or fashion courses can be via the same educational routes described above if they have the necessary background and ability, with particular emphasis on foundation courses. However, it is now more usual for mature students to gain entry via an Access course. These courses can be found at higher education institutions. Successful completion of the programme leads to a guaranteed place on the linked course.

Government has recognized Access programmes as the 'third route to higher education', alongside A levels and vocational qualifications. Students who have successfully completed a validated Access programme will receive a kitemarked Access certificate that enables them to apply to any higher education institution.

Further information and a complete list of Access courses in England is available from the Department for Education and Employment's despatch centre, PROLOG, on 0845 602 2260. For courses in Scotland, call the Scottish Office Education and Industry Department on 0131 244 0422, and for those in Ireland, contact the Department of Education in Northern Ireland on 01247 279643, extension 59699.

Many local adult education services offer 'portfolio preparation' classes. These may be useful if you are considering applying for further education courses or are preparing yourself for direct entry into higher education. Check with your local colleges and adult education services for availability.

Leather and footwear manufacture technology courses

There are relatively few providers of footwear and leather manufacturing courses. They are generally to be found in areas where traditionally shoes have been manufactured, such as the Midlands and Cordwainers College in the East End of London. These courses culminate in a National Diploma, Higher National Diploma (GNVQ Advanced) or a degree.

First degree in fashion, textiles and clothing (BA)

Degrees are not always vocationally specific. It is possible to take a combined art degree if you are not sure that you want to go into fashion and textiles. There are also specific courses in these subjects. These courses normally require three years' full-time study or four years' with an industrial placement.

Entry requirements: minimum age 18 on 31 December of the year in which the course begins: a BTEC Foundation Diploma; a BTEC or SCOTVEC National Certificate or Diploma; an Advanced GNVQ in art and design; an Access to Higher Education certificate awarded by an approved agency. Exceptionally, direct entry can be made with A levels or a Scottish Certificate of Education Highers.

An enormous range of first degree courses is available, usually specializing in either fashion or fashion and textiles. Courses are available in womenswear, knitwear, menswear, sportswear, clothing textiles, fashion promotion and illustration. Many courses combine business marketing and languages (usually

European ones, though not necessarily). For those students with more of a technical bias than a creative one, there are courses in clothing engineering and management, clothing marketing and distribution, marketing technology and even leather technology.

Postgraduate study – diplomas and higher degrees (MA, MPhil, PhD)

This level of study is offered at only about a dozen colleges or universities, covering areas of the fashion and clothing business and management, clothing technology and costume.

Entry requirements: normally completion of a first degree, although some courses will accept vocational and professional qualifications. Courses lead to certificates and diplomas or to higher degrees, such as MA, MPhil or PhD.

Postgraduate study falls into two distinct areas. The first extends your art education, perhaps leading to your specializing in one particular field, for example fashion menswear, fashion womenswear or knitwear. It may also be possible to choose a subject such as fine art, sculpture or jewellery after completing a fashion degree if your work develops such leanings. The second comprises courses that equip you for entry into special occupations, such as art teaching, art therapy, or arts administration, normally adding a professional year to your first degree qualification.

The Royal College of Art

The Royal College of Art has a worldwide reputation for the highest quality in all areas of its activities. It is the only entirely postgraduate institution of university status that is devoted to the study of art, design and communications. Courses lead to MAs and MDes. Full course descriptions can be obtained from the appropriate faculty of the college, but here are some examples:

- at the Royal College of Art Faculty of Design for Manufacture, courses are offered in embroidery, fashion knitwear, fashion menswear, fashion womenswear, knitted textiles, metalwork and jewellery, printed textiles, woven textiles;
- at the Royal College of Art Faculty of Design for Communications courses are offered in photography.

Professional qualifications

A large proportion of art education aims to train students for employment in specific professional areas of art and design.

Some courses, particularly at vocational level, have been set up with the approval of industries or professions that were consulted with regard to course content. It is possible, therefore, to gain two qualifications at the end of the course – an educational one and a professional one – which may be awarded after a special exam or by completing an additional year, in some cases by completing the course successfully.

The entry requirements for these courses may be agreed jointly by the college and the professional association concerned as the minimum for entrance to a particular profession. Some of the professional qualifications associated with art and design are:

CSD   Chartered Society of Designers;
LSDC   Licentiate of the Society of Designer Craftsmen;
ABID   Associateship of the British Institute of Interior Design;
BDS   British Display Society;
ATI   Associateship of the Textile Institute.

Journalism

The National Council for the Training of Journalists (NCTJ)
(see Chapter 4)

HND in journalism studies

This two-year course may now be taken at Napier University, Edinburgh. A limited number of graduates attend a one-year postgraduate journalism course at City University London, and University College Cardiff, before indenture.

All applications for one-year newspaper journalism courses are made to the NCTJ, not the colleges, except for the one-year postgraduate courses. There is also a one-year, full-time pre-entry course for potential journalists in the periodicals industry. Subjects include practical journalism, design, use of photographs and law. Entrants must have at least five GCE/GCSE passes, including English, and one at A level. The course is now run under the auspices of the Periodical Training Trust, Imperial House, 15 Kingsway, London WC2B 6UN.

Degree courses are listed in *British Qualifications* (published annually by Kogan Page). See also *Careers in Marketing, Advertising and Public Relations* (Kogan Page).

National Diploma

A BTEC HND in design (fashion) may be taken with an option in fashion writing at the London College of Fashion.

Photography

Proficiency Certificate in press photography

This qualification is awarded by the National Council for the Training of Journalists (NCTJ) towards the end of up to three years' provincial newspaper indenture and course attendance for trainee press photographers. Training is on the job and by doing full- or part-time courses. Course subjects include general photographic theory, law affecting press photography, caption-writing and practical press photography. Direct entry recruits to provincial newspapers need a minimum of five GCSEs at C grade or above, including English language. Often, trainees will have A levels or be graduates.

The NCTJ also runs a one-year pre-entry course. Application is through the NCTJ, Latton Bush Centre, Southern Way, Harlow, Essex CM18 7BL (tel: 01729 430009).

The following universities and colleges offer a number of courses in higher education that have options in fashion photography:

◆ Cleveland CAD: BA (Hons) in photography;
◆ Kent IAD: BA (Hons) in editorial and advertising photography; HND in editorial and advertising photography;
◆ University of Brighton: BA (Hons) in editorial photography;
◆ Wigan and Leigh College: HND in editorial photography.

British Institute of Professional Photography
The Institute awards a number of qualifications as follows:

◆ **Honorary Fellows (HonFBIPP)**
These are elected from among distinguished professional photographers.
◆ **Fellows (FBIPP)**
Fellowship is awarded for distinguished ability in professional photography. Fellows may describe themselves as an 'Incorporated Photographer' or 'Incorporated Photographic Technician'.
◆ **Associates (ABIPP)**
Associates must either have passed approved exams in photography with an appropriate period of experience or submit a thesis on an approved photographic subject. Associates may describe themselves as 'Incorporated Photographers' or 'Incorporated Photographic Technicians'.
◆ **Licentiates (LBIPP)**
Licentiates must be at least 21 and have passed approved exams in photography or have submitted evidence of their photographic or technical ability, having a minimum of three years' experience in professional photography. Licentiates may describe themselves as 'Incorporated Photographers' or 'Incorporated Photographic Technicians'.
◆ **Graduates**
These are students who have successfully completed a recognized course in photography or engaged in profes-

sional photography but not yet qualified, either by age, or experience, to take up corporate membership.

◆ **Student membership**
This is available for those pursuing a course in photography at an educational establishment.

◆ **Affiliate membership**
This is open to those who have a professional interest in photography, and because of age or other limitations have not yet qualified, or may be unable to qualify, for corporate membership.

Via the exam route, candidates may be admitted as licentiates on successful completion of the BIPP professional qualifying exam or an approved degree course.

Licentiateship may also be awarded to candidates with two years' relevant post-qualification experience following a recognized BTEC or SCOTVEC HND.

A recognized BTEC HND or C&G 744/745 Advanced qualification achieved by part-time study, together with three years' current professional experience which may have been gained during the period of study, may also lead to licentiateship.

Following a further period of professional experience and submission of examples of current work or appropriate evidence of technical ability, candidates may be awarded *associateship*.

How and when to apply for courses

For courses in art and design you may have to apply almost a whole academic year in advance of when you want to start. Details of when and how you should apply are laid out below. This is followed by some ideas on how to prepare for interviews and information on grants.

Most courses begin in the autumn. The dates and times given below refer to the academic year preceding the year of entry. It is very important that you use the most up-to-date reference books when applying, as details are liable to change over time. Applications for higher education courses are made via the Universities and Colleges Admissions Service (UCAS).

UCAS is the central agency handling all applications for entry to all UK full-time first degree, Diploma of Higher Education and HND courses. UCAS produces a yearly handbook, which is available from August of the following year. The handbook lists all courses, colleges and universities operating within the UCAS scheme and acts as a guide to application deadlines. Procedures are very rigid and UCAS insists that they are strictly adhered to. UCAS also has a Web site, the address of which is http://www.ucas.ac.uk

Foundation courses in art and design

There are both one- and two-year courses.

When to apply
From autumn to spring, normally to your local art college. Some popular courses will be full by January, so early application is recommended. There is no final closing date.

Method of application
Application forms are available from the colleges you are applying to and should be returned directly to them. It may be worthwhile to visit the college 'customer services' department in person. They will be able to advise you on availability of courses and local requirements.

BTEC First Diplomas and Certificates/GNVQ Intermediate

These are one- and two-year courses.

When to apply
It is advisable to apply from late autumn onwards, though some courses may have places available up until the late summer. There is no final closing date.

Method of application
Application forms are available from the college(s) and they should be returned to them directly once you have filled them in. For information on grants, see pages 44–45.

BTEC National Diploma/GNVQ Advanced

These are two-year coures.

When to apply

From late autumn onwards. However, these courses are particularly popular and those offering a specialist qualification in fashion and textiles will attract a large number of applications, so apply early.

Method of application

Application forms are available directly from the college(s) and should be returned to them. Your local authority may have rules on the payment of fees to colleges outside its area, so you should check with your local grants and awards department.

BTEC Higher National Diplomas/First Degrees in Art and Design

These courses take either two or three years to complete.

Method of application

Applications to universities and colleges are through the UCAS clearing system. This requires candidates to apply on a single form to all their course choices. There are two routes of equal status for application to art and design courses, which are Route A and Route B:

◆ **Route A**

Apply between 1 September and 15 December. As portfolio inspection and interviews need to be organized, you are strongly advised to apply by mid-November. Applicants for fine art at the University of Oxford should apply by 15 October.

◆ **Route B**

Apply between 1 January and 24 March. On later applications, the time is limited for portfolio inspection and candidates are required to indicate their availability for interview on a separate interview preference form.

It is possible to apply via both Route A and Route B. In this instance, you can apply for six courses, only four of which can be via Route B. If it is your intention to do this, then you will be asked to indicate that this is so on your application form so that UCAS can send on the additional documentation to add to your choices near the time.

UCAS charges a registration fee for processing application forms. The standard charge is £14. If you are applying for a single course at a single institution, you pay a reduced (£5) fee. If you decide to take this option, you may add other choices at a later date or enter clearing by paying an addtional fee of £9 (1999 rates).

Method of application
UCAS application forms and handbooks are available from your school or other educational institution you attend, your careers service and UCAS.

Other university degrees

The following information applies to a first degree in teaching and academic courses in art and design (such as the history of art).

When to apply
UCAS' and Oxbridge's closing date is 15 December.

Method of application
Via UCAS' clearing system. Six choices can be made on a single application form.

Other degrees at colleges of higher education

There are some courses that are not part of UCAS' system. This will be made clear in the prospectus and they are in the minority.

When to apply
From autumn onwards. There is no final closing date, but the popular courses do fill up quickly.

Method of application

As they are not part of UCAS, applications need to be made directly to the institution concerned.

Postgraduate study (higher degrees and diplomas in art and design)

When to apply

The necessary forms are available at the beginning of January. They need to be returned no later than the end of January.

Method of application

The application forms are available from your own college or, if you have already left, directly from UCAS. You may list two choices of institution. First choice interviews are held in February, while the second choice ones are in March.

Other higher degrees, diplomas and certificates at universities and colleges

When to apply

From December onwards. Many institutions have closing dates for postgraduate applications in the spring.

Method of application

Application forms are available from the postgraduate course, to which they must be returned.

Postgraduate art teachers' certificate/diploma and postgraduate certificate in education

When to apply

In the October prior to the year of entry.

Method of application

Application forms are available from the Graduate Teacher Training Registry. This operates a clearing scheme similar to that of UCAS. Four institutions are applied to on a single application form. There is a registration fee of £10 for processing the application form.

Access courses

These, you will recall, are for mature students who want to enter higher education.

When to apply

The dates of application will vary from one institution to another. Many Access courses are linked to particular universities or colleges of art. To check what is provided near you, contact your local career office. For a full list of all Access courses and a host of other helpful pieces of information, contact the Department for Education and Employment's despatch centre PROLOG on 0845 602 2260.

For information about Access courses in Wales, contact the Welsh Office Education Department (WOED). For courses in Scotland, contact the Scottish Office Education and Industry Department (SOEID). The equivalent in Northern Ireland – DENI – makes its own arrangements for the provision of further education.

Method of application

Application forms are available from the colleges themselves and should be returned directly to them.

Interviews and your portfolio

Whatever level of course you are applying for in art and design, you will be required to present a portfolio of work and attend an interview. The purpose of the interview is for staff at the college or university to meet you, look at your work and find out more about you. They will want to know your reasons for applying to that particular college and to decide on your abilities and suitability for the course. They will also want to find out what your motivation and interest in the course are.

Your appearance will matter. When applying for fashion courses, the way you dress should reflect your interest, either in terms of what you have chosen to wear or by the fact that you are wearing something you have made yourself.

Most importantly, you should be confident about your work. Your portfolio should reflect your personality and your abilities. Good preparation will give you confidence, so find out as much as you can about the college, the course content, methods of tuition and assessment, the facilities, options and subject choices.

Open days give you the opportunity to talk to students and staff and look around. If the college is not in your home town, try to look around the town too.

At some colleges – particularly at postgraduate level – you may be asked to sit an entrance test or exam.

The style of the interview will vary from college to college. It is possible that you will be interviewed in a group with other candidates or you may have an individual interview. Remember that the tutors responsible for admissions will be spending a considerable amount of time looking at portfolios and candidates, and so will be able to judge easily the level of effort you have put into your preparation. This is your opportunity to stand out. Art and design courses are unique in this respect. For many other courses in higher education, offers of places will be made entirely on the basis of school reports and exam grades, with no opportunity to sell yourself personally.

Before an interview, find out who can help you prepare both yourself and your portfolio. Your lecturer may know of a former student who has applied to that college and can enlighten you on the procedure, for example. You may be able to meet up with them at the open day or prior to the interview.

Tuition fees, funding, grants and awards

Government policies and legislation are changing all the time, so a book such as this may only serve as a guide. UCAS and your Local Education Authority (LEA) will be best able to advise you of the current position on further and higher education funding.

Since 1998, new entrants to full-time higher education who live in Britain have been expected to make a contribution of up to £1,000 per year towards the tuition fee costs of their course of study. Students on one-year sandwich course placements or those engaged for a year of their course in study or other experience abroad will be expected to make a contribution of up to £500 for that year of their course. These amounts are dependent on family income and so may be reduced.

If you live in England or Wales, your LEA will make an assessment of the actual amount of tuition fee payable. In Scotland, assessment will be made by the Student Awards Agency for Scotland. The Education and Library Board is the responsible body for Northern Ireland.

It is essential that you find out early about not only tuition fees but also your eligibility for grants and awards. You should make an application to your LEA or appropriate body in the spring before the course starts, even if you have not yet been accepted. There are two types of award – mandatory and discretionary – and the provisions of these are outlined briefly below.

Mandatory award

This is one that your local education authority is obliged to give you by law. You are entitled to this if you are taking a full-time degree course, BTEC or SCOTVEC Higher National Diploma or an initial teacher training course (BEd). You must be over 18 (on 31 December in the year of entry) and have been ordinarily resident in the UK for three years prior to the start of the course.

A mandatory award covers examination and tuition fees, plus a sum for maintenance (somewhere to live, food, books and travel). However, the sum awarded for maintenance was frozen in 1990. Since then, students have been offered loans to 'top up' the maintenance grants.

Discretionary award

This is one that the LEA may choose to grant. The criteria for such an award will vary according to the authority. These awards apply to both further and higher education.

Discretionary awards are modest and may only cover examination and tuition fees and some contribution towards travel costs. As they come from local funds, LEAs may be reluctant to finance students through a course in another area if it is on offer in their own.

Student loans

Students living in the UK are eligible to apply for a student loan from the Student Loans Company, 100 Bothwell Street, Glasgow G2 7JD, in order to fund their living costs while in higher education. The support available is assessed by the LEA (or their Scottish or Northern Irish equivalents) against family income. The loans are repayable after graduation, via the Inland Revenue, during the course of the remainder of your working life once your income has reached a minimum level. A graduate whose income falls below the minimum threshold at any time is able to defer repayments until their income level improves. Interest rates on loans are limited to the Retail Price Index (RPI), so that borrowers repay, in real terms, broadly what they have borrowed.

Non-UK residents are not entitled to apply for student loans. Student loans are not available to pay for students' contribution fees.

There are some special provisions made by government for students in particular circumstances: those with dependants, lone parents and those with particular hardships. The Government plans to introduce a supplementary 'Access' loan of £250 a year, available on a discretionary basis. Those who think they may be eligible should apply via their university or college and the Student Loans Company if they are suffering particular financial difficulty.

The Disabled Students Allowances (DSAs) Scheme is still available in the form of a grant to help meet course-related costs arising from disability. These allowances are not means tested.

Further details of the administrative arrangements for student loans are available from the Department for Education and Employment.

4 Career areas and jobs available

Graduates from the various fashion courses go on to enter a wide variety of occupations after leaving college. Most colleges and design centres keep detailed information about what jobs their students go on to do, so you could contact individual departments or college careers advisers if you wish to find out more. The Chartered Society of Designers and the Royal Society of Arts also have records of graduate employment, with periodic lectures and seminars by practising members and others.

What do surveys show?

A survey of art and design graduates carried out by Linda Ball showed that:

◆ art and design graduates take longer to establish themselves in a work role than graduates from courses in other subjects;
◆ 12 months after graduation, over 80 per cent of art and design graduates are in permanent employment or further full-time postgraduate study;
◆ 70 per cent are actively and positively involved with their art work.

This study lent support to the findings of the more extensive survey carried out by Ritchie *et al* (1972) *The Employment of Art*

College Leavers (HMSO). The survey found that, 12 months after graduation, nearly 80 per cent of art and design graduates were in work or further study related to the art and design field, but, in comparison with other graduates, they took longer to become established in their chosen field.

These findings have again been confirmed by a more recent survey, *Artwork* (1988), published by the Association of Graduate Career Advisory Services and carried out by its Art and Design Working Party. It examined the employment and further study patterns of art and design graduates shortly after graduation. It found that only 48 per cent were in full- or part-time employment and that 19 per cent of these also claimed to be involved in self-employment. Thirty-three per cent were unwaged, and 36 per cent of the unwaged also claimed to be in self-employment.

Many graduates take part-time or temporary work, not necessarily related to art and design, or register as unemployed while continuing to develop their artistic talents and build a network of professional contacts. They do this by writing letters, phoning around, making, and keeping, appointments, and then following up their letters and calls, which can be as time-consuming as a full-time job. This is a process and pattern that can often be followed for months before, eventually, you get the desired response – a job!

So what do fashion graduates do?

They go on to further study in art and design or further professional training, such as postgraduate courses – MAs and so on. Others find temporary work, often unrelated or only peripheral to fashion, while trying to establish themselves in self-employment, including freelance or consultancy work or setting up a studio or workshop. Alternatively, they find employment related to fashion but not necessarily design, such as sales, marketing or as a junior in the fashion department of a magazine or PR company. More often now, they go on to jobs in retail or design management that may also be open to all sorts of graduates but where having a design background may give them the required edge. Increasingly, too, they travel abroad in search of opportunities.

Whichever job you want to do, in general, the more highly qualified you are, the more likely you are to find a job. The achievement of a degree or diploma may combine with other personal skills and interests to equip artists and designers for careers in many fields, both related and unrelated to their course of study. For many art students, the opportunity to spend three or four years at college may have been an end in itself, an important stage in their personal development. Although this is less true for fashion and design students, the very nature of, say, a quality degree education does equip a graduate with an attitude and a frame of mind that is, by its very nature, flexible and adaptable.

Artists and designers have an important contribution to make in society and not only in art and design fields. They can show us how to be creative in a broader sense, and they can certainly use their creativity beyond their degree/diploma subject, as some of the case studies later illustrate.

What are the prospects?

Since the early 1980s, the whole country (and probably a large part of the world) has become more design-conscious. The economic growth in the 1980s brought more opportunities to spend money; remember that the 1980s saw the coining of the phrase (thank you, Peter York), if not the birth of, the 'Yuppie'! This in turn meant more opportunities for designers. All manner of products, not just clothes, acquired the 'designer' tag, from mineral water to bedlinen, kettles to calculators, hotels to pasta. The term 'designer' became commonplace. We became interested in improving the quality of our lives and, for some, our status, by the acquisition of consumer design products. Our fashion designers are lauded internationally. Abroad the big names have the status of royalty or Hollywood stars.

Retail companies in the 1980s, such as Next and Habitat, led to a renaissance for British retailers and manufacturers. The consumer boom created more opportunities, not only in design and production, but also in advertising, the media, the design of packaging and so on. The independent designers and crafts-people producing one-off and limited edition products were also enjoying a new recognition on this wave of design–aware spending.

Artists and designers became the new celebrities; they became more visible and achieved more credibility in society. Manufacturers have learnt the importance of design – that design sells – and now understand what they are paying a designer for. Forward-thinking companies have realized the benefits of designer/managers, of production and salespeople with design backgrounds. The business world is far more supportive of the arts overall. Government agencies sponsor design initiatives and foster an enterprise economy offering business support facilities and funding for small businesses, so that now, for example, artists, designers and craftspeople, on leaving college, can apply to the Graduate Enterprise Programme and for Business Starting Support (this succeeded the Enterprise Allowance) in order to establish themselves as small businesses.

Overall, it may be misleading to say flatly that employment prospects have improved for those undertaking fashion and, indeed, art and design education, but the broadening of the range of jobs now available does present a more positive situa-tion than in the past. However, this part of the job market is no less competitive than any other in a world where people are becoming better qualified. The effects of a world recession through the 1990s together with our own economic problems have taken their toll. The 'designer' world is more cautious and, despite the continual appearance of yet bigger, more stylish designer emporiums in our cities, it's a tough world when you're on the inside. Designers, like many others, partic-ularly in fashion and retail, have suffered unemployment, redundancy and a scarcity of freelance opportunities, so that the job market is now highly competitive and new graduates are competing for jobs with people who already have some experience.

The industry, though, like fashion itself, is constantly changing, never still, always on the move, adapting and responding to social change. It is in the spirit of evolution and social change that the fashion industry faces the challenges of the new millennium, with optimism and enthusiasm.

Postgraduate study

For many advanced courses it is often desirable, and sometimes compulsory, for applicants to have developed their work independently for at least a year after leaving art school. Funding for postgraduate study has diminished over the years, Department for Education and Employment bursaries being the main support for higher degrees and diplomas in art and design. In the first edition of this book, 10.5 per cent of polytechnic art and design graduates went on to postgraduate work (1979 leavers), compared with 7.3 per cent (1990 leavers – the latest figures available). Increasingly, in response to the shortage of finance, many postgraduate centres now accept applicants on a part-time basis for higher degrees and advanced diploma courses (see Chapter 3).

What skills do fashion graduates need to survive after college?

First of all, they should look at their own personal needs; then, at what skills and interests they have. What kind of career do they want – in the short and long term? In addition, they need to be:

◆ aware and well informed;
◆ realistic;
◆ self-motivated;
◆ flexible and adaptable to change;
◆ persistent;
◆ creative beyond their degree;
◆ professional;
◆ able to see fashion in a broader context than just clothes.

Recreating a college environment – by establishing a network of friends and contracts, grouping together with others, sharing skills and experiences, and joining artists' and designers' organizations – can help to counter feelings of isolation after college.

The Chartered Society of Designers holds regular portfolio surgeries with professional designers for its members. These take the form of friendly tutorials and can be invaluable for getting professional feedback on your work.

Most importantly, designers need to assess their skills and find ways of using them in other settings after college.

Fashion jobs

If at college you specialized in a particular fashion area – for example, menswear, womenswear, children's wear, promotion or knitwear – it is probable that you'll look for your first job in that specialism.

The breadth of employment opportunities is vast and varied and depends very much on your specialisms and preferences. Roles within the industry will vary considerably too, depending on the size and nature of a company. For example, a junior designer for a small British manufacturing company who supplies the high street with young fashionable separates may have a wide range of responsibilities within that role. These could be selecting and buying fabric, designing, pattern cutting, overseeing sample production, range building and selection, even negotiating with buyers. In a large international company, any one of those roles could be a job in itself. Sometimes in such companies an employee may have responsibility for just one particular garment area, such as soft tailoring, or even as specific as just 'skirts'. To specify all the job types would take another book and be somewhat pointless. To gain a good overall picture of the kinds of jobs that exist (and new jobs are being created all the time) and the skills required, regularly reading the trade magazines is probably the best option.

Your educational experience at college will broaden your knowledge and horizons of the industry and help you to decide where best you may contribute and find your niche.

Few careers work out as planned, life being a game of chance and opportunity; who knows what lies around the corner? Sometimes opportunities should be seized and others rejected – often the most difficult career decisions to make. There are many professional careers advisers with whom you can discuss your plans in confidence. Making a wrong decision can often set you back a long time, but this doesn't mean that you can't diversity, or equally, specialize or move sideways.

Case Studies

A look at the following case studies will reinforce these points, as well as illustrate how one job leads to the next. The most difficult job to get is probably the first and it is seldom perfect for you, but at least you're on the right track.

Andrew *left the Royal College of Art six years ago.*

'I was always interested in fashion and left school at 16 to take a GAD National Diploma course with a fashion specialization. At 18 I was accepted on to the BA (Hons) degree course at Nottingham Trent Polytechnic (as it was then). I felt I needed more time to develop my work and made a successful application to the RCA.'

He won a number of national and international awards and competitions while a student, and also worked both as a freelance and on placement during vacations as a designer and pattern cutter, the work varying from suppliers to mass market/high street stores in Britain and a high fashion designer label in Italy.

'On leaving the RCA at the age of 23, I was immediately offered a job in Germany working for an international fashion company. I turned this job down in favour of a job in England that offered broader experience working for a manufacturer supplying mass market multiples. The job involved fabric selection, liaising with buyers, creating and presenting theme boards, designing and personally cutting the selected designs, as well as overseeing the sample room production. Work was not seasonal and samples were produced continuously, with constant pressure always to include versions in the range of important and directional items seen on the international catwalks. From here I moved on to senior designer at Alexon International, where my work was varied and challenging. I worked within a large team, and became responsible for designing day and evening dresses and soft suitings, as well as researching for all areas, including tailoring and knitwear. The work involved compiling theme and mood boards for each season, selecting a colour palette, researching and liaising with both UK and international fabric agents, as well as designing. After doing specific drawings for the sample room, I would oversee the garments at toile stage, taking responsibility for the correct pads, buttons, zips, trims and so on. Finished garments were delivered to me before I presented them to my design executive.

I was also heavily involved in pricing meetings, fittings and organizing the finished range for the press shows and photographic shoots.'

A few years later – after moving on to other similar jobs and having completed several prestigious freelance commissions – Andrew decided the time was right to embark on a long-term dream to team up with an ex-colleague from his days at Nottingham – Reynold.

Reynold's *career had followed similar lines to that of Andrew – MA at Central St Martin's led to a design job with John Galliano, other industrial experience and, again, exciting freelance commissions. With an enormous variety of experience under their belts they thought they would complement each other perfectly and formed the label Pierce Fionda. They used all their joint resources and charm to raise finance and negotiate good deals for showing and selling their collections with the right people – contacts made while in employment. They were an instant success – so much so that they had to work very hard to get the clothes made to standard and delivered on time, and this was where their backgrounds really paid off. They see their periods in employment as a kind of apprenticeship, learning far more than they realized. This knowledge and experience is helping to underpin their future, which, judging from the success of their follow-up collections, is looking very rosy. In autumn 1995, they were chosen as 'New Generation Designers of the Year' by the British Fashion Council. Shortly after, they were approached by a high street department store chain, with whom they now work on a complementary diffusion line. This means that their work has become accessible to a wider customer base and gives them some financial stability for their main line.*

Bruce *After leaving school at 16 with only three O levels/CSEs, Bruce applied to Plymouth College of Art, where he studied for a DATEC Diploma in Fashion and Textiles.*

'Technically, it was a very good course. I feel I learnt more there about pattern cutting and garment making than on any following course.

I wanted to study for a BA and move closer to London, so I applied to Ravensbourne. Due to lack of school qualifications for BA requirements,

I was advised, while doing the DATEC, to take an A level. With this portfolio I was accepted for the BA course.

I studied at Ravensbourne for three years, but felt I wanted more time to develop my work, so I applied to the Royal College of Art to study for an MA. I graduated from Ravensbourne with a first and was accepted by the RCA.

I left the RCA in 1988, and my first job was at Donna Karan in New York. Two months after graduation, I was sent my work permits for the US and I moved over there.

My position with Donna was as design assistant on the newly launched DKNY line. My duties included garment design, toile fitting, jewellery and accessory design. After a year, I returned to London and was offered the position of design assistant with Bruce Oldfield.

Oldfield's business was made up of his couture line, diffusion line and various licensee work. I was mainly involved in designing a lower-priced diffusion line and knitwear, and womens' formal shirts and jewellery for the licensee accounts. I was with Oldfield for a year and was unfortunately made redundant. It was the early 1990s, the recession was biting and no full-time positions were around, so I went freelance. For over two years, I worked with Edina Ronay, Liberty and Trussardi. This work usually involved just design work on paper, although at Edina and Liberty designs were followed through garment stage. At this time I also did wardrobe and styling for TV commercials.

Through friends I was asked to design the wedding dress for Serena Stanhope, which I undertook as a freelance commission. It was the first royal wedding for some time and attracted a lot of media attention.'

Shortly after, Bruce got the opportunity to work with another top British designer, Amanda Wakely, whom he assists, working on the ever-increasing range and on special projects.

Some fashion-speak explained

Before continuing with the case studies, it is necessary to explain further a few areas and terms related to the industry.

Wholesale

This, essentially, is everything that happens before goods are sold to individual customers (the buying public). In the fashion industry, jobs concerned with this directly would include that of production manager, for example, but, of course, strictly speaking, all design and sourcing jobs are also wholesale.

Retail

Retail is selling to the public. Large retail companies (such as big store groups) often run structured training courses. Trainees usually start with selling 'behind the counter' or 'on the shop floor' and move up either into department (and maybe eventually store) management or go on to train as a buyer.

In small shops – for example, exclusive designer boutiques – the training is usually less structured, but then it probably doesn't need to be structured, as individuals' interests, personalities and talents are easily spotted within the comparatively small staff teams. A buyer's job may require travel, often overseas, and may involve working with factories and designers on product development.

Marketing

Essentially, marketing provides a link between the manufacturer and the retailer/customer. It involves: research and analysis of general fashion trends and of the market competition; product planning to make sure that the garments produced meet a demand and continue to do so; and sales forecasts, advertising, public relations and promotion. Marketing directors will oversee all these functions in large operations, with people working under them in speciality areas. In small companies, marketing managers or directors will deal with these functions personally.

Large companies and advertising agencies offer their own management trainee schemes and sometimes schemes specifically geared to marketing, but competition for traineeships is fierce.

The Communication, Advertising and Marketing Education Foundation (CAM) is an educational charity, originally formed from the educational sections of the Advertising Association, the Institute of Practitioners in Advertising and the Institute of Public Relations. As the industry's examining body, it is supported by 14 organizations in the communications field. Its certificates and diplomas are nationally recognized qualifications.

Tuition is available on full-time courses, part-time day or evening classes, and correspondence courses. Full details of the scheme can be obtained from Abford House, 15 Wilton Road, London SW1V 1NJ (tel: 0171 828 7506).

The Chartered Institute of Marketing courses include a two-year, part-time certificate course with exams in June and some-times in November. Those who pass may then go on to take a one-year, part-time diploma course. The programme is at present under consideration and may change. Details are available from Moor Hall, Cookham, Maidenhead, Berkshire SL6 9QH (tel: 01628 427500).

Merchandising

This is a much overused term. Usually, and strictly speaking, it is the marketing or targeting of products to particular customers or to particular sectors of the consumer market. This is where merchandising overlaps with definitions of marketing. For many companies, particularly since the 1980s' consumer/ design boom, this has become big and sophisticated business. Unlike marketing, there aren't courses specializing in merchandising, but because of the blurring of definitions, a marketing course linked to fashion business studies would probably be close in some aspects. However, the best route would probably be to complete a design-based course, almost all of which incorporate such studies these days as part of the business programme.

Here is yet another example of an alternative career route for those interested in careers in the fashion industry, where design awareness and understanding are more of a prerequisite than actual design abilities. The old definitions of 'wholesale' (design, production, and so on) and 'retail' have become blurred in these areas as information not only on fashion trends but also on spending and 'lifestyle' trends, competitor reports and others are continually fed back and forth between one and the other.

We are living in an age when *how* you sell something is as important as *what* you are selling. In large companies, the marketing department would work alongside designers, buyers, merchandisers and PR teams; now sometimes all these people are incorporated into one team, which may have an umbrella title, such as product development.

Case Studies

Elizabeth, from an early age, knew she wanted to be a 'dress designer'. She did a foundation course at Gloucestershire College of Art, which, after A level art in a repressive girls' school, seemed like a wonderful new world opening up. She was asked to stay and do fine art, but, single-mindedly, she wanted to pursue her fashion interests, so it was on to a fashion and textiles degree at Middlesex Polytechnic (as it was then). The course was very broad, even covering accessory design.

'I think this helped make me more of an all-rounder. I went on to the Royal College of Art, which I had always wanted to do, and feel that, although I found it less "enjoyable" than Middlesex, it was what I needed: a bit more time to gain confidence, and to learn to work with "real" companies in the outside world.

I did knitwear for my degree show and consequently found my first job in Paris doing the "young" range for part of a large, internationally known design company. I hated this job and soon returned to London. By this time it was September and all the jobs had gone, so I took my own collection to a small shop opening up off the King's Road. They bought it *all*, so I had to go home and reproduce it in quantity. I was too "green" to form a proper business, so literally worked for myself and managed to support myself for a year. Despite full orders books, press coverage in *Vogue*, and *Harpers and Queen*, etc, I decided to wind it up, having worked myself into the ground and fallen ill.

I found a job as a knitwear designer in a small family business supplying high street multiples. This brought valuable experience working with factories and manufacturers. I had to prepare ranges, sketches, specs, colours and yarns for production in Britain and Hong Kong.

This was followed by a brief stint at Mr Freedom, back working with woven clothing again, and on to assistant designer at Sally Tuffin, where additional experience was gained in the areas of fabric buying, sampling and selling, and dealing with customers and responding to their reactions.

Then came a knitwear design job at Deryck Healey International – a textile and fashion consultancy. I produced designs and knit samples for contracts in Japan and the US. I landed up as head of the women's fashion department, in charge of a team of designers working on various contracts and trend information for clients such as ICI, Goya Perfume, Fashion Folio Publications, Woolworth Clothing and Woolworth South Africa.

I was asked by Design Intelligence, a trend information service, to set up its womenswear department. The company sold books of designs and ideas worldwide and offered consultancy to jeanswear manufacturers. Again I stayed in this job five years and between these two I learnt about company policies, planning and politics, as well as management. I was also invited to teach part time at Bristol, Derby, Preston and Kingston.

Restless at not seeing clothes made up first-hand, I joined the Next company as designer/buyer, where I learnt about colour selection, fabric buying, price negotiation, range-building and working with manufacturers in the UK and Hong Kong. Tired of very long hours and travel between Leicester and London, where I lived, I moved to Conran Design Group, working on consultancy retail projects, producing designs and presentation boards one year ahead of the selling season.

A chance meeting with Next personnel at a colour and fabric fair in Paris led to my being asked back to work as design manager of a small team of designers setting up the *Next Directory* as well as working on ranges for the stores. I learnt a whole new discipline of how to put a mail-order catalogue together. When the director and initiator of the whole Next chain, George Davies, and his wife were ousted in a boardroom coup, I decided I'd had enough of fashion. I opted for a complete change and went for a year to horticultural college and became a gardener at Hever Castle for two years. I couldn't make ends meet and genuinely missed fashion, so looked for another job.

I went to Marks & Spencer as a freelance designer and feel my consultancy and retail experience helped greatly as we work almost like consultants for our own company. There are about six designers and one co-ordinator in womenswear. We put together a large design brief for buyers and manufacturers at the beginning of a season (one year ahead) then work with our individual departments. We watch over the process of first samples from manufacturers to production samples. The organization is so big that there is always a great deal of learn about the running of it and all the different departments, and the 'profiles' of different stores throughout the UK and Europe. In addition, there are regular meetings and presentations to the various ranks and management.'

Ann studied fashion design at Middlesex College of Art (now Middlesex University) after completing a foundation course in her home town of Liverpool. She went on to study for her MA in womenswear at the Royal College of Art. Her first job was with a company in the centre of London's 'rag trade' in the West End. After six months, she started her own design company with a friend. They designed a range of womenswear, produced the samples and sold to prestigious London boutiques and American stores via the buying houses.

The partnership lasted four years. It was very hard to make enough money for two people out of one small business, so they decided to part amicably. The partner specialized as a skiwear designer and Ann then went on to design lingerie freelance for a friend and colleague who had a fashionable lingerie label called Tuttabakem. After a few years as a freelance designer for a variety of clients, she now works for a lingerie company that supplies Marks & Spencer with lingerie and blouses. Ann's responsibilities now are looking after a small team of designers based in London and co-ordinating with the factors in South Wales.

Her job involves liaising with selectors from the multiple stores who give some indication of the merchandise they want for forthcoming seasons, directing the team of designers to design exciting but commercial products, presenting the final designs to the selectors and co-ordinating the range. She has to work with fabric, lace and embroidery companies to develop new materials and colour stories, and oversee the factories' interpretations of her team's original samples. Ann must also liaise with the commercial executives to make sure the garments are within cost. Regularly, Ann visits trade fairs in Europe and make trips to shops and stores in European cities to keep abreast of trends at all market levels.

Lynnette, before going on to study fashion at degree level at Kingston Polytechnic (as it was then), did a one-year, pre-diploma foundation course, which stood her in good stead for the demanding rigours of a degree. After college she went initially to Italy to look for work, but found things were not quite as easy as she'd hoped.

She returned to London and worked for three months as a sales assistant, where she learnt about sales systems and gained an understanding of retail, which was to prove beneficial later.

After three months, Lynnette was offered two jobs at once. She took the one working as womenswear designer/fashion forecaster for a large fashion design consultancy. This led on to a job with a major jeans company and to Lynnette specializing in menswear, which she does now for one of the most important fashion design consultancy and forecasting companies in Britain.

The company produces a range of trend forecast books aimed at different market sectors. Each book includes: design ideas and sample specifications; colour fabric stories and ideas for themes; labels, packaging and styling – all of which Lynnette has to contribute to as part of a team that includes people with graphic design, womenswear, knit and textile specialisms.

The company also offers individual design packages for clients and part of the job entails managing a number of projects simultaneously. Lynnette has to laise with clients about projected work and communicate *with, and organize, not only the in-house team but also freelance designers and illustrators who are used for special projects and roles.*

As trends emerge from ever broader sources, the job involves lots of travel to the various influential fashion fairs and centres, where Lynnette has to keep a close eye on the newest and emerging trends.

Suzanne, *now a product and design development manager for a company that is part of the largest textile group in Britain, began by taking a one-year arts foundation course, followed by a BA Honours degree in fashion and textiles at St Martin's School of Art. For three years, she worked as a handknit designer as part of a design team for a major yarn spinner. She designed men's, women's and children's garments for magazine editorials, patternwork and hardback publications.*

'I organized photographic sessions and proofread the knitting pattern copy. I also made presentations of the company's designs to customers and magazine knitting editors.

Then I took a four-year studentship at the Victoria & Albert Museum in textiles conservation. This involved learning about chemistry, solvents, textile construction and researching the objects.

After that I returned to design, managing a knitwear shop and overseeing the production of the garments for the shop and for export to the US. This gave me experience dealing with outworkers, yarn producers and the buying public, which is vital in my present position.

I liaise with garment manufacturers, fabric suppliers, chain store selectors and with my company's own production, sales and development departments. I act as a translator, as it were, between our customers, designers and our own technical staff. I visit major fabric and yarn exhibitions and am always looking out for new processes and effects that we can adapt and develop.

Another part of my job that I have been keen to develop is closer links between industry and education.I am involved in local school projects and I'm part of an industrial liaison committee at a local fashion college where I have been the external assessor for two years.

My job is really varied, never the same two days running. I meet lots of people at all levels within the industry.'

Nicky *studied for a BA in textile design, specializing in knitwear, at the Scottish College of Textiles for four years.*

Through the Royal Society of Arts she won a placement with Courtaulds. The placement turned into a 14-month job assisting in designing ladies' knitwear for production in the Far East. The job entailed swatching knit and embroidery ideas, garment design, liaising with customers and trips to the Far East, New York and Paris. She felt, however, that she needed more in-depth knowledge of the fashion side of design and applied to the Royal College of Art to study for an MA in fashion knitwear. There she learnt all aspects of fashion design, more about working with industry and how to tackle several varying projects simultaneously.

After graduating, Nicky worked with a friend on a number of freelance jobs, which included costume for television, shop styling and window display, and fashion research.

Nicky has recently set up her own business with two colleagues. They design and sell knit swatches for the US, European and Japanese markets. They also work with design duo Pierce Fionda to produce their complementary knitwear range, which is produced in Italy.

Clare's *background is in textiles, but her current senior position as print designer at Marks & Spencer, as part of a six-person womenswear design team, is a perfect example of where the skills of both fashion and textiles designers are required in one person.*

Clare left school in Hull with one A level and eight O levels and took a pre-diploma foundation course in Sheffield before going on to Birmingham College of Art (as it was then) for a BA in fashion textiles, specializing in printed textiles.

'My first job was design assistant to Pat Albeck, a design studio in London. My first responsibilities included developing colourways and design repeats for fashion, furnishings and giftware, not to mention dog-walking and general dogsbody, but I learnt lots and found it an excellent introduction to London.

After about a year, I moved on to a design assistant post with Veronica Marsh Print Studio. We produced fashion print collections for the US market. When I had been with them for three years, I became responsible for sales direction for Veronica Marsh Studio in Paris. A year later, in 1978, the company was working with the Japanese market. I visited Tokyo, Kyoto and Osaka and became partner to Veronica Marsh, selling in New York on the studio's behalf.

In 1980, I left the studio to work solo until 1981 when I was offered a job with Walker Rice Fabrics, London, to design and sell the print and woven fabric range. In 1983, I joined Nigel French Design Consultancy, where I was responsible for presentation and input to production packages. Twice-yearly visits of a month's duration to Australia and New Zealand enabled me to co-ordinate them with our US customers. I had to make work presentations at least once a day.

In 1986, I was offered a full-time post at Brighton Polytechnic (as it was then) as principal lecturer for printed textiles and course leader for fashion textiles, responsible for departmental, staff/student timetabling and general course structure, reporting to the head of department. In 1989, restless to return to the industry, I accepted the offer of a post at Marks & Spencer. In 1991, I was given responsibility to create and establish the womenswear colour palette.

My main tasks are to research colour and pattern trends one-and-a-half years in advance of the season and to communicate it to the rest of the design team, womenswear management and selectors. I also co-ordinate all the womenswear departments. Part of the job involves travel to research worldwide retail trends and to the major textile fairs, including Expofil, Pitti Filatti, Premier Vision and Interstoff.'

Magazines, journalism and fashion writing

In fashion terms, the title 'journalist' is generally misused and usually refers to a 'fashion writer'. Fashion writers usually have their own specialist qualifications, although, occasionally, a local newspaper or general interest magazine may use a 'regular' journalist to contribute fashion stories as well as other news stories.

Journalism

The traditional way to start in newspapers is with a small local or provincial paper, where you train under a training contract or during a period of indentured employment leading to a National Certificate or NVQ/SVQ at Level 4. Some companies have their own in-house training schemes that may also be open to employees of other companies. From there, you can graduate to one of the larger circulation provincial papers in one of the big cities, such as Glasgow, Birmingham and Liverpool, and so work your way up to the national press.

Like many other careers that sound glamorous and are popular choices for school-leavers, journalism is difficult to get into because there is a great deal of competition. The hopeful recruit must keep a sharp look-out for a suitable job as a trainee in the situations vacant section of the local press (including the free press), as well as the national and regional newspapers. Check details of new jobs in the media section of the *Guardian* every Monday, the *UK Press Gazette*, *Media Week* and *Campaign*. The *UK Press Gazette* – which is available on subscription but can also be ordered through a local newsagent, has more advertisements for jobs in journalism than *Campaign*, which is produced primarily for the advertising and publicity world.

You may also be successful if you write directly to the editors of local and regional papers on the off-chance that they may be able to take you on rather than wait for a job vacancy to be advertised. Your local library should have up-to-date copies of *Willings Press Guide* or *Benn's UK Media Directory*, which list all the newspapers and periodicals, together with their addresses.

Training in newspaper journalism is more rigidly controlled than in periodicals or magazine journalism, with qualifying examinations to be passed and courses to be attended. Most trainees are direct entrants – that is, they are given on-the-job training combined with day release or block release college courses.

School leavers who want to join a newspaper's training scheme are advised to apply to a paper in their area. Minimum entry qualifications are five GCSE passes (grades A–C) or equivalent, including English language. Some newspapers may also require one or two A levels or three Scottish Highers, or equivalent, one in English.

Over half of the entrants to newspaper journalism are university graduates, relevant disciplines being history, politics, economics, English, law and classics. However, there are some entrants with exceptional talent who are taken on with no special academic qualifications.

Another way is to apply to the National Council for the Training of Journalists (NCTJ) for a place on its one-year, full-time pre-entry course. The Council's address is Latton Bush Centre, Southern Way, Harlow, Essex CM18 7BL (tel: 01279 430009). A small number of accredited colleges and universities (a list of them is available from the NCTJ) offer one-year courses in newspaper journalism. To qualify, you need at least two A levels or equivalent and two GCSEs, all four in different subjects, or three Highers, including English and two O grades. Apply to the NCTJ, enclosing a 23 × 109 centimetres (9 × 4 inches) stamped addressed envelope. Applicants who are considered suitable must attend a day of written tests and, if successful, attend an interview.

In magazines, some companies will have their own training policies. Magazines use a high percentage of freelances, reflecting their goals of offering newness and variety.

It is important to apply early to your LEA for a discretionary grant, so that you can find out what your financial situation is as soon as possible. When writing to the LEA, the full designation of the course must be quoted. For example 'Full-time professional pre-entry course for newspaper journalism, DfEE registration number 355-7009 on course list 209. It is an "advanced" course within the terms of the Further Education Regulations 1975.'

A number of the top fashion magazines run annual competitions for young 'wannabe' writers. Success in such competitions can mean exposure, work placements and even job opportunities.

Don't forget that you may be lucky enough to find a newspaper company that will agree to sponsor you on a full-time course, although this happens only in exceptional circumstances.

After the course, students need to find a trainee vacancy on a provincial newspaper and will serve an 18-month qualifying period before taking the National Certificate examination. During this time they may be assessed for S/NVQs either as well as or instead of taking the examination for the National Certificate.

Some newspaper groups have their own in-house training schemes that meet the NCTJ requirements. Graduates apply in the same way as school-leavers. One-year postgraduate diploma courses in journalism are available.

Further information is included in *Careers in Journalism* (8th edition, Kogan Page).

Fashion writer

It is generally agreed that, while fashion magazines and fashion pages in newspapers may look slicker and better than ever, the quality of actual fashion writing has sadly deteriorated. Many writers currently appear to be historically ill-informed, lacking in any sort of political (with a small 'p') conviction or awareness and concerned with little more than enthusing over fashion's latest darling. Perhaps you could be part of a new generation able to bring back some quality to this area.

Fashion writers usually – although they could conceivably come via a journalism course – have a design background.

Having gone through a series of traditional design education courses – GAD or foundation and so on, and on to an HND or degree – many people find that knowing how to design, cut and sew, and how the industry runs gives them a good, sound background that also includes visual and critical studies as a platform for their own visions and opinions.

A few courses are now emerging at colleges with an already established, broad portfolio of courses, specializing in fashion writing and journalism. These should be seriously considered as alternatives to more traditional journalism courses and may save a year or two of separate training.

Stylist

The name alone is enough to give this job popularity and glamour, but opportunities are just as scarce as in many other areas of fashion and equally competitive. As elsewhere, flair and talent have to be matched by professionalism and a sound knowledge of how the industry works. The usual route is, again, via traditional fashion education. Few actual full-time jobs exist, most stylists being employed on a freelance basis or, as is the case with magazine work, where writing and reporting may also be involved.

Most stylists begin by being assistant to a stylist, which may involve very menial work: collecting clothes, accessories and so on from PR companies, finalizing booking with hairdressers, make-up artists and models; ironing and pressing clothes; organizing lunch and refreshments for the crew on a shoot, and so on.

The kind of work open to stylists includes that for magazines on promotional material such as brochures and publicity shots, for fashion shows and events, and, of course, in the music business. Sometimes styling overlaps with display and often freelances do both.

Magazines are put together approximately three months before publication date, so stylists need to be 'in with the in crowd', absolutely up to the minute and beyond. They need to know everything, and everyone, that is happening, constantly looking ahead for what is new and possibly influential.

Case Studies

Andrea arrived in England from New Zealand to study fashion, having completed her school studies and worked in various jobs for a couple of years. After one year on a BTEC fashion course, she realized the course was not demanding enough of her and would therefore not equip her for her future plans. Aged 24, she switched courses to study BA (Hons) at Nottingham Trent Polytechnic (as it was then). She graduated in 1989 with what she now realizes were quite unrealistic ideas about the job market and of fitting into the 'working world'. She was 'unable to get a job within a company that she was prepared to see past those naïve student ideals'. She started making her own clothes, selling through friends and contacts in London and Manchester for about a year.

Andrea then landed a junior position with a London PR company, which she found interesting and challenging, learning skills she had until then only touched upon. She stayed with the PR company for one-and-a-half years, but eventually felt frustrated at not using her creativity. Through her contacts she approached Sky magazine and offered to work two days a week for free in order to understand the workings of the fashion department. After a few months, she was offered the position of contributing editor, bringing to the department her interest in menswear.

Having arrived the hard way, Andrea realizes the importance of being helpful and willing to 'muck in'. She thinks many students and graduates feel a lot of work is beneath them.

Andrea's day varies depending on what is happening in the office. She has made a short list of some of the jobs involved in organizing a shoot:

- booking a photographer – which may involve calling in portfolios to look for an appropriate style;
- booking a model – which may involve a casting (models call this a 'go-see');
- appointments to view collections;
- selecting, and hopefully booking, garments and accessories;
- booking hair and make-up – often similar to booking a photographer and involving portfolios;
- styling 'looks' once garments are all in before the actual shoot;
- the shoot – transport for team and clothes may also have to be organized;
- returns and merchandising into the computer the prices, stockists, and so on.

The idea and possible budget for the shoot are discussed with the editor before the go-ahead is given.

Andrea has recently returned to New Zeland to work on launching a new fashion magazine project, which shows that it pays to keep up contacts wherever you end up in the world!

Sally *became one of the fashion editors of Britain's top-selling, glossy women's monthly magazine,* Marie Clarie. *She began her specialist training with a three-year degree course in fashion at Nottingham Trent Polytechnic (as it was then). After the first year, she realized that her strengths lay in compiling stories (series of fashion photographs in magazines linked by a theme) and styling clothes to create a look. The degree course did not cater for any alternative careers except design (although she did get encouragement and support from staff), so she wrote to* Elle *magazine to see if they would take her on an unpaid work placement for a month. At* Elle *she spent a week on the telephone in the merchandise department getting prices for clothes that had been photographed. Then she asked if she could work in the fashion department and spent a month assisting the fashion director, telephoning, packing up clothes and doing appointments. Sally also entered* The Sunday Times' *Young Journalist Competition and won.*

After completing her degree course, Sally took a year out to travel and, while in Australia, she worked for three months 'helping out' on Australian Vogue. *Sally thinks the best way to find work is to be very keen and use your initiative. Work is not as glamorous as people think and a lot of time is spent bagging up clothes and on the telephone – she says she's spent many a midnight alone in a clothes cupboard! If you are passionate and diligent, all the hard work could pay off.*

After a brief stint assisting at The Sunday Correspondent, *Sally landed the job of junior fashion editor at* Marie Claire *and was responsible for the '101 Ideas' pages for two years. She then felt the time was ripe for a change and worked as the stylist for* The Independent *for a year. By then she had gained much more experience and knowledge and was asked by* Marie Claire *to come back as fashion editor. There she was responsible for main page stories and travelled to wonderful places. However, the job, although more exciting and fulfilling, became more and more demanding and Sally worked long days and evenings and had to sacrifice many weekends, although, in her own words, she loved what she had to do enough for that to be a small price to pay.*

Organizing a shoot involves first thinking of a story or concept – often based on a favourite film, book or artist – and then deciding which photographer will be suitable and together choosing the model, hair and make-up artists they think most appropriate. Finally, they choose a location – it may be a hotel, studio or a beach in Africa, depending on the clothes, season and the budget available.

The team consists of a photographer, photographer's assistant, fashion editor, make-up artist, hairdresser and model. Once on the shoot, a large part of the job becomes keeping everyone happy – making cups of tea, massaging the photographer's ego and making everyone laugh and feel relaxed. A good team spirit is essential to producing the best pictures. You have to be passionate about what you do and work towards the same goals.

One of the satisfying aspects is being inspired by the brilliance of the designers, then reinterpreting their looks in your way with accessories, and directing the hair and make-up to take the original concept of the designers a step further.

Fashion photographer

In fashion, there is always the person who hasn't arrived via the usual routes, the usual college background. In the sphere of photography, it is often the irregular route that is the norm. There are probably more successful fashion photographers who haven't come to it via a college background than those who have. This, quite probably, is because it is one of the few areas left that has something of the remains of an old apprenticeship system, where young photographers can complete their training and gain professional practice working as photographers' assistants.

There are a number of photography and a few specialist fashion photography courses within the BTEC, HND and degree systems, but, in addition, there are courses organized by the British Institute of Professional Photography, which include technical and creative aspects of professional photography. Most fashion degree courses include some photography – at least as an option – and it is often this, coupled with a sound fashion education and basic grounding in photographic technique, that has led to a 'sideways step' into the role of fashion photographer. All fashion photographers are freelance. Very rarely, they may work under contract to a large client, but this is still, strictly speaking, a freelance arrangement.

Runway or catwalk photography

The photographers are collectively known as 'the pack'. They either work directly for a magazine or newspaper, or freelance, taking the pictures, then approaching the press in the hope of selling the photographs and recouping their costs. In short, they feed the fashion press with fashion news.

A runway photographer works 'on the road' for approximately four months of the year. Twice a year for about two months at a stretch they will shoot *haute couture*, ready-to-wear and the international menswear shows. There can be up to 12 shows a day – the first often at 9.00 am, the last maybe around midnight. The photographers' day starts almost as early as the models'. They have to be at the show venue approximately two hours before it starts to be assured of a prime spot. In between shows, they have all their equipment to carry and masses of spare film to move from venue to venue. Also, they often have to send film off to labs to be developed in time to make the news headlines.

Advertising and editorial photographers

Magazines, newspapers and other clients commission these photographers. They work either from a studio or on location. While it is common for editorial photographers both to work from a studio and to do location work, it is highly unusual to find one who would do runway photographs. Equally, runway photographers extremely rarely also do studio or location work – except, perhaps, in the early years of their career when they might be experimenting across all areas or simply helping make ends meet. Unless they are very well established, advertising and editorial photographers will hire studio space by the day as this is much cheaper than having it on a permanent basis. This is because when photographers have their own studios, the costs fall to them, but when a studio is hired, the cost falls to the client. These days, photographers often hire their equipment too, as good, basic equipment could set you back £50,000, and different work (location, studio and so on) requires different equipment (camera, lights, lenses, for example). Having said this, most photographers do own some basic equipment themselves.

For some jobs, a photographer will require an assistant, whose role will include setting up cameras, lighting and other equipment, backdrops and settings, loading cameras, checking light readings and so on. They may also be responsible for keeping the studio tidy or, on location, for packing and transporting equipment, running errands and being a general gofer! Again, unless they are very well established, photographers generally hire assistants by the day.

Work for magazines, advertisements and promotion is

usually gained via an agent, who will arrange the booking, fee and all the business arrangements. For this service, an agent will take 25 per cent commission. A very successful photographer may employ a person to do all the work an agent would do – arrange bookings and so on, take control of the office, sell work and take portfolios about. For this, an assistant would be paid a salary and a small commission.

The Association of Photographers produces a factsheet entitled 'So you want to be a photographer?' that provides job outlines, advice on making contacts with photographers, how to present your CV and information on suitable photographic courses and qualifications. To obtain a copy, write to the Association of Photographers Limited, 81 Leonard Street, London EC2 4QS, enclosing an SAE. The Association's telephone number is 0171 739 6669.

Most top fashion photographers started by being assistants to other top fashion photographers after they completed their education and training – hence the similarity to apprenticeships.

Part of the deal in being an assistant to a photographer is that, in return for looking after and tidying the place, he or she can use the equipment and studio. Another perk is that the company that prints the photographer's work processes the assistant's film for free or half price.

Case Studies

James has an art school background. He did an art and design diploma (equivalent to a BA) in fashion design at what was then called the South West Sussex Art School, then went on to the Royal College of Art to study millinery at MA level. In those days, the course was three years long, but, after two years, he left to set up his own company. This was in the 1960s and London still supported the last of the breed of British couturiers – Norman Hartnell. Ronald and Michael Patterson were important fashion figures. Ronald saw James' hats in a show at the RCA and asked him to make hats exclusively for him. His next break was when Liberty approached him and set him up in business with a workroom, with the proviso that they had first choice of all his designs.

It wasn't long before he had a name for himself, but he felt restless to move on. He set up on his own with a studio in Ganton Street – in the heart of London's fashionable Carnaby Street area.

As one of the designers contributing towards London's bright young image, he was soon at the heart of fashionable society. His hats were constantly being photographed for fashionable magazines – Vogue, Harper's Bazaar *and so on. He came to know all the photographers – David Bailey, Terence Donovan and Duffy. He liked them, liked their work, and liked the life. He already knew all the models as they wore his hats in photographs and real life. He also knew Suzannah York, as a customer and friend, and she sold him a second-hand camera belonging to her husband.*

That was it. He seized the opportunity, packed up the business in Ganton Street and found a studio in the City. He struck a deal with the landlords whereby he would do up the place if he could have six month's free rent.

He started practising, using the models he knew and his hats, but it was two years before his first work came along. He had been feeling very low, very disappointed, when Meriel McCooey, then fashion editor of the Sunday Times *colour supplement rang up and commissioned him. James wanted to do something very new, and had been experimenting with hand-colouring black and white photographs, so this is what he did. They were a huge success and from them other jobs came flooding in, all wanting tinting because at this time no one else was doing it.*

For a while he became pigeon-holed and found it difficult to break-away and move on. James realized that while he wanted to develop his work and change, certain characteristics have to remain so that work has recognizable, subtle, personal qualities, such as his own personal fashion awareness, his own taste. James thinks it is important for a fashion photographer to be aware not only of fashion, but also the look of the model:

'A lot of successful photographers are known for the types of model they use – it is a very important relationship. It is important to recognize personal taste in order to create your own personal look, your own images. This enables you to move on; you are inspired by heroes, etc., but you have to use that feeling to allow your own personality to come through, being creative, experimenting with lighting, techniques, equip-ment, etc, and always re-evaluating work.'

He thinks very few photographers are every totally satisfied with their finished work. The whole concept of what goes through the mind, what you see, and what the camera produces means that, when you see photographs, they are not quite as you visualized them. At the same time you have to be open-minded and susceptible to the unexpected, to chance. He thinks you have to be very selective and that the 'technical side is important; it is important to understand it, but then forget about it'.

James recommends that anyone who wants to be a fashion photographer should be an assistant first, even if they have done all their schooling, obtained a degree, and so on. It was a lot easier when he started off and he is not sure his method would work today.

James does all his own black and white developing. Most photographers send their developing out today, but he feels strongly about doing it himself as there is so much you can do to the image at this stage, and good developing should be part of the creative process.

Anthea *works primarily as a freelance catwalk photographer covering the women's ready-to-wear shows twice a year in Milan, London, Paris and New York.*

'I sell my pictures around the world on a non-exclusive basis. I have the privilege of viewing the top and the newest in designer and model talent.

As with many photographers I did not have formal training, but switched one visual profession for another. At college, I took a foundation course and then opted for a degree in illustration, concentrating on super-real renderings for general subject matter. Gradually, more interest developed in fashion.

For a year directly after college I freelanced. Some skill, no contacts and little practical experience do not add up to a successful formula.

I was given the opportunity to work full time illustrating and researching for a fashion consultancy and learnt various aspects of the industry. Quite by chance, the photographer hired to cover shows for us did not appear. Consequently, a camera was handed to me to 'take some pictures'. I had the luxury of learning, especially technically, on the job with no financial responsibilities and the added bonus of a fashion background. I knew what was of consequence and the importance of composition.

Ten years on, this has become a more sophisticated and difficult profession to be involved in. A major publication with a high circulation is the only guarantee of entry to the collections. The right equipment and back-up means constant investment. Work is at specific points in the year and the conditions as well as the schedule require tremendous physical and mental stamina. Being a freelance, commitments must come upfront in order to make a trip viable. Each season is usually a month's duration. Film costs (approximately 700 rolls!), processing and travel expenses are footed by the individual in advance. This is a vast outlay and explains one of the reasons why this is a difficult speciality to get into. Multinational, multilingual, exciting, competitive and challenging – the best and only way to break into this is to assist, paid or unpaid, and learn the ropes.

As with a lot of careers in fashion, it's deemed to be glamorous. Far from the truth, this is the most gruelling work but somehow addictive! The quality of the work is just a part of what the profession is about. Editors need to know who you are. Self-promotion is necessary. Who you are and, who you know are as important as how well you photograph.'

Illustrator

Fashion illustration is yet another area where traditionally specific training has not existed. Most successful fashion illustrators trained as fashion designers by way of degree courses. Most people will confirm that, having gone through the rigours of conventional, design-based degree courses, the would-be illustrator not only has a rounded view of the whole industry and the illustrator's role within it, but also a sound understanding of garment construction, fabrics and the body. However, in response to the growing recognition that there are many valuable roles within the fashion industry that require a knowledge and appreciation of design but not necessarily actual design ability, a number of colleges are now offering fashion illustration options, usually as part of fashion promotion and communication courses. The actual 'weighting' of fashion illustration varies from course to course and is best revealed by careful scrutiny of the course handbooks themselves.

There are few (if any) full-time jobs for fashion illustrators; most work freelance. Some design jobs require particular illustration skills, but most people recognize that it is extremely rare for people to excel at both illustration and design. Personal interest and talent usually lie within one area or the other, although all design jobs do require a level of competence in illustration.

Work for illustrators comes usually from designer/manufacturers, forecast and consultancy companies and magazines and the press. Many fashion illustrators find that by extending their repertoire to include exercise illustrations, make-up and cosmetics, they can gain more work.

As the final illustration is usually the last stage after the actual design process, it is often left until the last minute and illustrators find they often have to work to very tight deadlines, juggling previous commitments and cancelling social plans. As with any freelance work, payment is usually negotiated beforehand, maybe per individual drawing or for the whole job, never by the hour.

In order to help them receive a steady flow of work, many illustrators employ an agent. The agent will usually keep colour photocopies or slides of a selection of the illustrator's work on file. When clients show interest, they may ask to see the whole portfolio. Again, as with all freelance work, you are not paid for time or expenses to tote your portfolio around. An agent may take up to 25 per cent of your fee as commission. This, too, should be negotiated fully when you enlist the services of an agent. The Association of Illustrators, 1st Floor, 32–38 Saffron Hill, London EC1M 8FH (tel: 0171 831 7377), can supply a list of agents specializing in fashion work.

Case Study

Judith left her home in Yorkshire to complete a one-year foundation course at St Martin's School of Art. Although she always knew that she wanted to follow a fashion course, Judith found the foundation course was an extremely good introduction to all aspects of art and design with lots of opportunities to experiment in other areas. After foundation, she chose to stay on to study for her degree at St Martin's because, at the time, it had a very strong illustration department. She enjoyed designing, but was already more interested in illustration.

While still at college, Judith was offered her first job with the design consultancy company Deryck Healey International. At that time, the company covered fashion, textiles and interior design and employed 70 full-time designers. She was employed as designer/illustrator in the knitwear department. Her job involved working on special design projects for manufacturers in Australia, South Africa and the United States. Judith regularly travelled to Paris and Italy for the collections and trade shows for trend news and inspiration. After her first year, she became one of the full-time illustrators, working for the womenswear and menswear studios. She met and worked with many people at DHI who now work for major companies – ICI, Courtaulds, Marks & Spencer – and have since given her freelance work.

After five years with DHI, she was made redundant and so began an enforced freelance period. Judith worked mainly for magazines and publishers at this time, doing beauty and cookery illustrations with very *little fashion. After two years, she was tempted back into full-time employment by an opportunity with another major fashion consultancy, Nigel French, to work as reports manager. Her responsibilities included organizing retail and trade fair reports for clients around the world, to keep them up to date with European trends. The reports themselves involved research, writing copy, editing and illustration as well as delegating to a team of designers and illustrators.*

After four years in this role, Judith felt restless to move on, opted to go freelance and has been working from a studio at home for the past seven years. Still working for all the major fashion consultancies and manufacturers, she also works for magazines in the areas of fashion, beauty and cookery and has even done educational illustrations for publishers of encyclopaedias.

Judith also teaches part time at Derby University, Nottingham Trent University (formerly Nottingham Polytechnic) and Epsom School of Art.

Judith says the advantages are control over your time and the amount of work you want to do and when you do it. Despite the disadvantages that work frequently has to be chased and that it is difficult, if not impossible, to plan your finances, on the whole she much prefers working freelance.

Fashion model

There are two main areas of work for fashion models – photographic and catwalk. Models for the latter are more often these days called runway models. Very often people do both kinds of modelling.

There are no specific academic qualifications for becoming a model, although obvious basic GCSEs (or equivalent) are recommended as a base for simply getting through life. Girls must, however, be a minimum of 5 feet 7 or 8 inches tall and usually have hips no larger than 35 inches. Boys must be at least 5 feet 11 inches tall. Someone of exceptional looks who doesn't quite fit these minima may get photographic work. You must have very good, clear skin and should be able to maintain your weight easily. Ever since the 1960s and the advent of models such as Twiggy, there has been a market for very young female models; it is quite common for girls to begin modelling at 15 years old.

It is not necessary to attend expensive modelling school courses, although it may help deportment and personality development.

In order to obtain bookings for work, models have to have agents who work as managers and bookers on their behalf. The majority of top modelling agencies are in London, where most of the work is. A few have provincial offices. Anyone considering this type of fashion career is advised to make an appointment to see an agency, preferably one with a good reputation, approved by the Association of Model Agents, The Clockhouse, St Catherine's Mews, Milner Street, London SW3 2PU (tel: 0171 584 6466). An information line is available for those interested in modelling careers: 0891 517644 (premium rate).

Newspapers and magazines are always making headlines publishing how much money top models make. These are generally the élite few. More realistic speculation is difficult, but an agency would be able to advise better, looking at each model individually. You should realistically expect to spend the first year learning to be a good model and the second making money. Career expectancy is about five to ten years. Male models traditionally have a longer working life, although at present there is a trend – let's hope not short-lived – for more mature female models as well as the bright young things.

Having got an appointment with a model agency, you should bring along snapshots of yourself – but do not go to the expense of studio shots – a good agent should be able to tell at a glance whether or not you have potential. An agent may ask you to sing a contract – as with any such legal document, do not sign anything until you have discussed the situation with your family or your family solicitor. Once they have enlisted you, the agency may well tell you to do something with your hair, have a tooth capped and so on.

Some agents have deals set up. For example, a fashionable hairdresser may do your hair in exchange for your doing hair shows or publicity shots for them, a local gym or health club may offer you discounted membership or a young, up-and-coming photographer may take test shots that you can each use for your respective portfolios and 'cards'. Cards are the show cards (usually approximately A5 size) with a selection of a model's best photos, showing, ideally, a variety of 'looks' and giving details such as name, agent, address and personal statistics. These are sent or handed out to prospective clients for reference. Sometimes an agent may send you for a fresh reel of photographs; the cost of this can be negotiated.

It is quite usual for you to spend the initial few months using up what seems like all your money on photo tests, hair and make-up, and learning how to relax and feel comfortable in front of the camera.

There is no proper 'new model' rate, other than the regular hourly rate, but, as with experienced models, clients will often negotiate a fee with the agent and the model for a complete job. There may be times when the chance to model for a particularly fashionable designer, photographer or a prestigious client, or get exposure in a TV commercial, for example, may be more beneficial in the long term than the immediate 'money-in-the-bank' factor. Once enlisted, the first booking may take quite a while to materialize, maybe a few months, and even after the first few jobs, work may still be erratic. Many young models subsidize their income at first by doing other part-time work. The most successful models do runway shows and photographic work. The designers, you may remember, only show twice a year generally, so outside of the collections, time can be filled doing other work.

An agency generally takes 20–25 per cent of a model's earnings as its fee. There are two methods of payment: for 20 per cent, the model must wait for the client to pay the agency the fee; for 25 per cent the model receives 60 per cent of the earnings 10 days after invoicing the agency and the remaining 15 per cent after the client has settled the bill.

Models are required for editorial publications, TV commercials, advertising catalogues, fashion shows and sometimes promotion work.

Case Study

Thea was discovered by her agency, Directions Models, while she was shopping on the King's Road and has been with them for six months. She was approached by a scout from the agency when she was 15. Her mother was invited to the agency with her, where a career as a model and what was expected were explained in great detail. Thea made the decision to join and was immediately tested by several photographers and able to start building a portfolio. She had the advantage of being a child actress and felt confident in front of a camera.

The agency styled her and taught her how to do her make-up. She has her hair looked after by a top hairdresser, free of charge. Thea says:

'My agency also taught me to walk for the catwalk and I have now done many shows, which are very exciting. I am also very lucky because I am naturally thin – the camera does add pounds. It is a very exciting career and I work with very interesting and creative people, but it is hard work rushing around town everyday on 'go-sees' and castings. I have been very lucky in the short space of time and have done a lot of editorial work.'

The agency has just secured a contract for Thea with a Japanese agency. She will be going for two months and hopes to earn a lot of money and gain valuable experience. She hopes, then, to work in Europe and internationally.

Costume and wardrobe

Usually costume designers will be expected to have had training and a background in courses specifically oriented towards the needs of theatre and costume drama (see *Careers in the Theatre*, Kogan Page). Wardrobe, though, is another area where the skills of a fashion-trained person may be more appropriate – a knowledge and understanding of the fashion history, a good eye for fashion detail, trends, and so on. A TV programme may be made 3–6–12 months in advance, a film is more likely 12–24 months. That the characters look completely contemporary and up to date may be essential to the credibility of the whole production. The necessary skills for costume and wardrobe, though clearly related, may vary considerably.

One of the biggest areas of employment is television. It is more often the case that people move from TV to film than start from scratch in film, owing to the simple fact of scale. However, one way to do this is to work on commercials, many of which are, made by film people between major projects. In commercials, the wardrobe person usually works alone (is free-lance) and having been briefed by the director and maybe other significant members of the team or crew, will go and buy the clothes or have them made up. Sometimes wardrobe people make clothes themselves; where the budget allows the wardrobe person may have an assistant.

In television, the costume design team usually consists of a costume designer, costume design assistant, senior dresser and dressers. They will usually work on a variety of projects that may range from drama and period drama through to light entertainment.

The beginning for someone wanting a job in costume or wardrobe (after education) is usually as a costume design assistant. Such a person is required to assist the costume designer in all areas of the job, and duties undertaken are to maintain contact between artistes and suppliers, arrange fittings, carry out the necessary research and background work, source fabrics and so on. An assistant is the deputy for the costume designer.

The costumer designer begins with the script for a production and, together with the producer, director and choreographer, will read, analyse and decide on an interpretation of the text of the script in relation to the artiste, sets and so on. They have to work to the agreed budget for the production and handle people firmly, yet with diplomacy. They have to be able to work in a team and communicate ideas and requirements effectively. Qualifications for costume designers and assistants are usually a BA Hons in theatre design or fashion, or equivalent.

The duties of dressers include the maintenance of costumes and dressing of artistes for performances. They need sewing skills and preferably some experience in theatre, theatrical costumiers or film.

When costumes are made, this is done by dressmakers, who are expected to work on a variety of garments ranging perhaps from futuristic styles, through period to sets of dancers' costumes. Working to designs and drawings, they make their own patterns, then cut and prepare garments for fitting and completion. Basic training in pattern cutting and garment production to BTEC Higher National Diploma in clothing or fashion is essential.

Case Study

Jane *is a costume assistant with the BBC. She has worked on a number of shows, one of which is Jennifer Saunders' hilarious spoof of the world of fashion PR,* Absolutely Fabulous, *co-starring Joanna Lumley.*

'I did a one-year foundation course at Mid-Warwickshire College of Education from 1977 to 1978 and did a BA (Hons) degree in fashion and textiles at John Moores University in Liverpool. I did not really know what I wanted to do when I went to art college, but I was interested in theatre and the performing arts, so I thought I could combine both by doing costume in either theatre or television.

I did a short period of industrial training at BBC Manchester and at Granada television studios, which I enjoyed so much that I decided then to try to get into that side of things.

I applied to the BBC many times without success. It was only when I had worked as a costume maker at Cosprops Ltd, a very well-respected costumiers, for three years (where I learnt about pattern cutting and garment making) that I was able to gain the relevant experience and was successful in getting a post as a dressmaker in the workroom at BBC television in 1986.

From April 1989, I started working as a costume assistant and have worked on *Eastenders*, *Russ Abbot Show*, *Bread*, *Brushstrokes*, *French and Saunders*, which led to *Absolutely Fabulous*, *Newman and Baddiel* and *House of Elliot*, where I was costume adviser/assistant. This involved doing drawings, making toiles and costumes for the dummies and teaching the girls in the workroom how to sew!'

5 Getting started

It has never been easy to get a job, and probably never harder than today. You have to be realistic, keen, determined and even energetic. You have to be good.

Getting a job is almost a skill in itself. The most difficult one to find is probably your first proper job. Many graduates tell similar stories of how hard they worked at college to obtain a good grade pass, only to discover that what an employer really wants is proof that you can do the job required – in short, experience. If you are applying for creative jobs, employers like experience, but they also want the freshness of a graduate bursting with ideas and creativity – shades of catch-22 perhaps. It is often a frustrating time, those first few months after college, toting your portfolio around, interview after interview, trying always to be bright and keen.

Of course, there are always the lucky few who are offered jobs while still at college – but how does this happen? Sometimes scouts from major employers visit degree shows; sometimes students may have been spotted while involved in an externally set project, a placement with a company or have had their profile raised by winning a competition or bursary.

If you were not one of the lucky ones; you were not offered a job before you left college, term has ended and you are out there, what do you do? Where do you start? Obviously you read all the trade papers and any of the quality nationals that may publicise details of the kinds of jobs you are interested in, but where else can you look? There is a small number of agencies that specialize in employment recruitment for the fashion trade, some of which you may have heard about while at college. It doesn't cost anything to register with them, visit them and discuss the nature of the position that will suit you, and it still doesn't cost you if they find you a job.

Employment and recruitment agencies receive a fee (usually based on a percentage of your first year's salary) paid by the employer. So do not hesitate to call them up, introduce yourself and make an appointment to discuss your future career aspirations ASAP.

An agency will advise you on your portfolio and help with you CV – these days the look and format is unfortunately as important as the content. Go to see all the recruitment agencies – the more people who are out there looking for a job for you, the better! Be frank and honest about your aspirations and be receptive to the advice of these professional recruiters, but remember too that you have to promote yourself. This is no time to hide your talent. Be positive, assertive, optimistic and enthusiastic. Sell yourself, just as you have to with a potential employer; in this respect think of them in the same light. You need to look, act and be professional. Think of interviews with recruitment personnel as practice for actual job interviews and if you are unsuccessful with an interview, again be positive – it is good practice for the next interview.

If you hear of a job and wish to apply for it, do your homework! Research the company, find out what you can about it (if you feel it is necessary for the post offered, go to your public library as it will hold company reports). Read what you can about it in magazines, find out stockists (if you do not know them already) and go and look at the current range. Analyse the company carefully, thinking who the customer is, price points, the competition and so on. Ask around for information from friends, contacts and others. This knowledge will help you to present the right image at interview. Ask for a job specification from the company before you go to the interview, so that you can be sure to offer what is wanted and ask the right questions.

How else can you find a job? You can ask around. Again, ask everyone you know – friends with jobs; people you knew at college; maybe people who were a year above you who have contacts and experience; tutors and staff. As long as it is done professionally there is nothing wrong in asking people you've been involved with at college through projects and so on. You could ask people in the industry if they could spare half an hour to see you, to look at your portfolio and give you advice, rather like a tutorial. To gain that valuable experience to put in your CV, you can always ask to work for a week or month or so for free and, as some of the case studies testify, the important point is that people know you are out there looking for a job. In the end, it is very much the old case of being in the right place at the right time.

Portfolios

If you are seeking a design job or a position that requires creative skills, you will need to show a portfolio of your work. If you have just left college, you will have had help from tutors in preparing this, but if it is some time since you left, your portfolio will almost certainly need updating. In fact, your portfolio should never be static; it will need constant updating and editing with fresh new work slotted in to replace other dated or weaker pieces.

People in employment often never think to keep a record of work done, or don't have the time, but it is worth making the effort to keep colour photocopies or get copies of photographs and so on of work you feel is particularly successful or significant in some way. People freelancing often find themselves in a similar position, in a rush to send work off on time to a client and, before they know it, left with nothing in their portfolio to prove they ever did it! If you have a budget from the client for materials for a job (which you can often negotiate), you can sometimes include copies of your own work, so records cost you nothing. Illustrators can occasionally get the originals back from the client after they have been used (this sometimes happens with magazine work).

As a general rule, do not include old work. Your portfolio should read as fresh, new and exciting. However, if you feel that a particular piece of work is testament to a particular ability not represented elsewhere in the portfolio, it would make sense to incorporate it.

When applying for a specific job, your portfolio selection should be tailored to the job requirements – another example of where thorough researching of the company can be beneficial. At the actual interview, too, you can be confident knowing your relevant abilities and experience are reflected in your portfolio selection and are apparent to the interviewer. It can be beneficial to set yourself a small project aimed at the company interviewing you, to show them that you can 'fit in' and are capable of producing the right work for them.

It is always a good idea to make sure that your portfolio includes some black and white drawings that can be faxed anywhere in the world to an interested potential employer wishing to gain a flavour of your work and abilities. A black-and-white version of a piece of work can be completed alongside a colour drawing or design. After drawing out the work, but before adding colour, photocopy it and complete the black-and-white copy with tone only.

The Chartered Society of Designers regularly holds 'portfolio surgeries' for its members, where volunteer professionals will offer you advice and direction. These are arranged both in London and in the regional offices; dates are published in the Society's journal, *Preview*, and, if you are a member, it is well worth taking advantage of these opportunities.

6 The future of fashion

Where is fashion going? This is a question akin to asking what the future has in store, to which there are, of course, no firm answers, no more so than any of the questions we might ask about what the next millennium may hold for us.

The future of fashion, like the future itself, is what we make it. In the future, fashion will change, just as fashion itself will change the future. To understand change, you have to understand the moment. Fashion is a reflection, a product, of its time. Fashion designers, or, indeed, anyone creatively involved with fashion, need to be as aware and as well informed as possible of what is happening in fashion and in the spheres that affect fashion.

The media today is so extensive, so up-to-the-minute, that fashion is reaching and responding to more people than ever before. Fashion at the moment is riding on a high – never has fashion been so popular, so fashionable even, and there seems no foreseeable reason for this popularity to abate. There is more air-time devoted to fashion, with several regular and many special TV programmes. It seems almost daily that another magazine or fashion-related company launches itself on the Internet. Fashion personalities, designers and models are the stars of TV commercials and the celebrity guests of chat shows and interviews. Fashion shows are calendar events, the subjects of documentaries and provide the 'plots' for commercials and drama. A recent newspaper article described a model as giving the ultimate post-modernist performance, a performance that was completely devoid of content. Food for thought!

It is an exciting and glamorous world, but one of much more than tinsel and glitter. Fashion and its related industries rank third in the list of Britain's biggest employers – it is big money. If you look around the world and count not only the glamorous fashion design capitals but look at Asia and India, say, you can start to imagine the scale of, and scope for, the industry's employment possibilities.

Fashion is a social phenomenon and, like society itself, it is diverse. The breadth of trends is now vast – gone for good are the days of one look for everyone, the equivalent of a 'one size fits all' fashion story. Fashion now is far more democratic, spanning age and class in ways that not too long ago would have been unthinkable. Fashion's inspirations and manifestations are coming from ever more diverse and esoteric roots, its changing cycles blurring the tracks of its ephemeral references.

Fashion is about more than what is the new black, the length of a skirt or the width of a trouser hem, it is a mirror of society, its preconceptions, obsessions and shifting opinions. Tom Wolfe's 1980's quip, when asked about his own individual style of dress, is now perhaps truer than ever: 'the way we dress is the most honest thing we ever say about ourselves'. Today, and for the foreseeable future, what we wear really does reflect who we are, or give indications, signals, to those in the know. To know what we will be wearing in the future, maybe we should be asking ourselves who we will want to be.

One thing we can sure of is that there will always be fashion and a fashion industry as long as we still have something to say about ourselves, and fashion will change as long as invention and novelty have anything to do with it.

The world of fashion is vast, boundless even, it needs the skills of many to exist, it offers scope for all ranges of talents and abilities and, because of its constant evolution, there will be an ever-broadening array of employment opportunities.

7 Useful addresses

General

Arts Council of Great Britain, 14 Great Peter Street, London SW1P 3NQ (tel: 0171 333 0100; fax 0171 973 6590)

Arts Council of Northern Ireland, 181 Stranmillis Road, Belfast BT8 5DU (tel: 01232 381592)

Arts Council of Wales, Holst House, Museum Place, Cardiff CF1 3NZ (tel: 01222 394711)

Chartered Society of Designers, 32–38 Saffron Hill, London EC1N 8PH (tel: 0171 831 9777)

Crafts Council, 44a Pentonville Road, London N1 9HF (tel: 0171 278 7000)

Department for Education and Employment, Publication Centre, Westex, PO Box 2193, London E15 2EU (tel: 0181 533 2000; fax 0181 533 7700)

Department of Education in Northern Ireland, Rathgael House, Balloo Road, County Down, Northern Ireland (tel: 01247 279643)

Design Council, 34 Bow Street, London WC23 7DL (tel: 0171 420 5200)

Design Council (Scotland), Ca d'Oro Building, 45 Gordon Street, Glasgow G1 3LZ

Design Council (Wales), QED Centre, Main Avenue, Treforest Estate, Treforest, Pontypridd CF37 5TR

Edexcel Foundation, Customer Enquiries Unit, Stewart House, 32 Russell Square, London WC1B 5DN (tel: 0171 393 4444)

Scottish Arts Council, 12 Manor Place, Edinburgh EH3 7DD (tel: 0131 226 6051)

Scottish Office Education and Industry Department, Victoria Quay, Edinburgh, Scotland EH6 6QQ (tel: 0131 244 0422)

The Welsh Office, Training and Education and Enterprise Department, Central Services, Companies House, Crown Way, Cardiff CF4 3UT (tel: 01222 380753; fax 01222 222885)

Further Education Division, Welsh Office Education Department, Third Floor, Cathays Park 2, Cardiff, CF1 3NQ (tel: 01222 826616)

Regional arts boards

Eastern Arts, Cherry Hinton Hall, Cherry Hinton Road, Cambridge CB1 4DW (Bedfordshire, Cambridgeshire, Essex, Hertfordshire, Lincolnshire, Norfolk, Suffolk); tel: 01223 215355

East Midlands Arts, Mountfields House, Forest Road, Loughborough, Leicestershire LE11 3HU (Northamptonshire, Derby, Leicestershire, Nottinghamshire); tel: 01223 215292

London Arts Board, Elme House, 133 Long Acre, London WC2E 9AF (tel: 0171 240 1313)

Northern Arts, 10 Osborne Terrace, Newcastle upon Tyne NE2 1NZ (Tyne and Wear, Cleveland, Cumbria, Durham, Northumberland); tel: 0191 281 6334

North Wales Arts, 10 Wellfield House, Bangor, Gwynedd LL57 1ER (Clwyd, Gwynedd, Montgomery District); tel: 01248 353248

North West Arts Board, 12 Hartet Street, Manchester M16 6HY (Greater Manchester, Merseyside, Derbyshire (High Peak), Lancashire, Cheshire); tel: 0161 228 3062

South East Arts Board, 10 Mount Ephraim, Tunbridge Wells, Kent TN4 8AS (Kent, Surrey and East Sussex); tel: 01892 515210

South East Wales Arts Association, 9 Victoria Street, Cwmbran, Gwent NP4 3PJ (Cardiff, Gwent, Mid Glamorgan, South Glamorgan, Radnor and Brecknock Districts); tel: 01633 875075

Southern Arts, 13 St Clement Street, Winchester SO23 9DQ (Berkshire, Buckinghamshire, Bournemouth, Poole and Christchurch, Isle of Wight, Hampshire, Oxfordshire, West Sussex, Wiltshire); tel: 01962 855099

South West Arts, Bradninch Place, Gandy Street, Exeter, Devon EX4 2LS (Avon, Cornwall, Devon, Dorset (except Bournemouth, Poole and Christchurch), Gloucestershire, Somerset); tel: 01392 218188

West Midlands Arts, 82 Granville Street, Birmingham B1 2LH (Hertfordshire, Worcestershire, West Midlands, Shropshire, Staffordshire, Warwickshire); tel: 0121 631 1321

Yorkshire and Humberside Arts, 21 Bond Street, Dewsbury, West Yorkshire WF13 1AX (Yorkshire, Humberside); tel: 01924 455555

Professional organizations, private colleges and other useful addresses

Acme Artists' Housing Association Limited, 44 Copperfield Row, London E3 4RR (tel: 0181 981 6821)

Advertising Association, Abford House, 15 Wilton Road, London SW1V 1NJ (tel: 0171 828 2771)

Art Services Grants and Space, 6 & 8 Rosebery Avenue, London EC1R 4TD (tel: 0171 278 5139)

Art Workers Guild, 6 Queen Square, London WC1N 3AR (tel: 0171 837 3474)

Art Workers Management Limited, La Berry Place, London EC1V 0JD (tel: 0171 608 1403/0171 490 4499)

Association of Artists and Designers in Wales, 54b Bute Street, Cardiff CF1 6AF (tel: 01222 464576)

Association of Degree Courses in Fashion and Textiles Design, c/o Sally Wade, Department of Advanced Studies in Art & Design, Bradford & Ilkley Community College, Great Horton Road, Bradford BD7 1AX (tel: 01274 753264; fax 01274 753236)

Association of Exhibition Organisers, 26 Chapter Street, London SW1P 4ND (tel: 0171 932 0252)

Association of Illustrators, First Floor, 32–38 Saffron Hill, London EC1N 8FH (tel: 0181 752 5252)

The Association of Model Agents Limited, 122 Brompton Road, London SW3 (tel: 0171 548 6466)

BBC Corporate Recruitment Services, White City, Wood Lane, London W12 7TS (tel: 0181 752 5252)

Bristol Old Vic Theatre School, 1–2 Downside Road, Bristol BS8 2XF

British Antiques Dealers Association, 20 Rutland Gate, London SW7 1BD (tel: 0171 589 4128)

British Association of Art Therapists, 11a Richmond Road, Brighton, East Sussex BN2 3RL (an information folder costs £5, send an SAE for list)

British Display Society, 70a Crayford High Street, Dartford, Kent DA1 4EF (tel: 01322 550544)

British Fashion Council, 5 Portland Place, London W1N 3AA (tel: 0171 636 7788)

BTEC (Business and Technology Education Council), Central House, Upper Woburn Place, London WC1H 0HH (tel: 0171 413 8400)

Byam Shaw School of Art, 2 Elthorne Road, London N19 4AG (tel: 0181 281 4111)

CAPITB Trust, 80 Richardshaw Lane, Pudsey, Leeds LS28 6BN (tel: 0113 239 3355)

Careers and Occupational Information Centre (COIC), Moorfoot, Sheffield S1 4PQ (tel: 0114 259 4563)

Careers Research and Advisory Centre (CRAC), Sheraton House, Castle Park, Cambridge CB3 0AX (tel: 01223 460277)

Central Services Unit for Careers and Appointments Services, Crawford House, Precinct Centre, Oxford Road, Manchester M13 9EP (AGCAS careers literature and vacancy information for graduates) tel: 0161 237 5409

Christie's, 63 Old Brompton Road, London SW7 3JS (tel: 0171 581 3933)

City and Guilds of London Institute, 1 Giltspur Street, London EC1A 9DD (tel: 0171 294 5409)

The Communication, Advertising and Marketing Education Foundation, Abford House, 15 Wilton Road, London SW1V 1NJ (tel: 0171 828 7506)

Designers' and Art Directors' Annual, 9 Graphite Square, Vauxhall Walk, London SE11 5EE (tel: 0171 582 6487)

The Further Education Funding Council, Cheylesmore House, Quinton Road, Coventry CV1 2WT (tel: 01203 863000; fax 01203 863100)

Independent Television Commission (ITC), 33 Foley Street, London W1P 7LB (tel: 0171 255 3000)

Institute of Medical Illustrators, c/o Angus Robertson, Medical and Dental Illustration Unit, Leeds Dental Institute, Clarendon Way, Leeds LS2 9LU (tel: 0113 233 6258)

Institute of Packaging, Sysonby Lodge, Nottingham Road, Melton Mowbray, Leicestershire LE13 0NU (tel: 01664 500055)

Institute of Practitioners in Advertising, 44 Belgrave Square, London SW1X 8QS (tel: 0171 235 7020)

Institute of Scientific and Technical Communicators, Kings Court, 2–16 Goodge Street, London W1P 1FF (tel: 0171 436 4425)

London Enterprise Agency (Design Enterprise Programme), 4 Snow Hill, London EC1A 2BS (tel: 0171 236 3000)

Museums Association, 42 Clerkenwell Close, London EC1R 0PA (tel: 0171 608 2933)

National Artists' Association, Interchange Studios, Dalby Street, London NW5 3NQ

National Association of Decorative and Fine Arts Societies, 8a Lower Grosvenor Place, London SW1W 0EN (tel: 0171 233 5433)

National Council for Vocational Qualifications, 222 Euston Road, London NW1 2BZ (tel: 0171 387 9898)

Riverside Studios, Crisp Road, London W6 9RL (tel: 0181 741 2251)

RSA Examinations Board, Progress House, Westwood Way, Coventry CV4 8JQ (tel: 01203 470033)

Royal College of Art, Kensington Gore, London SW7 2EU (tel: 0171 584 5020)

Rural Development Commission, 141 Castle Street, Salisbury, Wiltshire SP1 3TP (tel: 01722 336255)

SCOTVEC (Scottish Vocational Education Council), Hanover House, 24 Douglas Street, Glasgow G2 7NQ (tel: 0141 248 7900)

The Sheldon Trust (Community Arts), The Old Tin School, Colyhurst Road, Manchester M10 7RQ

Society of Designer Craftsmen, 24 Rivington Street, London EC2A 3DU (tel: 0171 739 3663)

Society of Graphic Fine Art, 9 Newburgh Street, London W1V 1LH

Society of Scottish Artists, 69 Promenade, Portobello, Edinburgh EH15 2DX (tel: 0131 669 0637)

Society of Typographic Designers, 21–27 Seagrave Road, London SW6 1RP (tel: 0171 381 4258)

Sotheby's Works of Art Course, 30 Oxford Street, London W1R 1RE (tel: 0171 323 5775)

Student Loans Company, 100 Bothwell Street, Glasgow G2 7JD (tel: 01345 300900)

Textile Conservation Centre Limited, Apartment 22, Hampton Court Palace, East Molesey, Surrey KT8 9AU (tel: 0181 977 4943)

Textile Institute, 10 Blackfriars Street, Manchester M3 5DR (tel: 0161 834 8457)

United Kingdom Institute for the Conservation and Restoration of Historic and Artistic Works, 6 Whitehorse Mews, Westminster Bridge Road, London SE1 7QD (tel: 0171 620 3771)

Fashion recruitment services

Austin Knight, 20 Soho Square, London W1A 1DS

Craig Vigler Associates Ltd (Star Executives), Lloyd Street, Manchester M2 5WA (tel: 0161 839 3387; fax 0161 831 7202)

Denza International, 11 St George Street, London W1R 9DF (tel: 0171 499 5047; fax 0171 629 8376)

Fashion Personnel, also **Executive Personnel**, Circus House, 21 Great Portland Street, London W1P 7FD (tel: 0171 436 0220; fax 0171 436 0088)

Freedom Recruitment, 50 Great Malborough Street, London W1V 1DB (tel: 0171 734 9779)

In-Design, 1 Ashland Place, London W1M 3JH (tel: 0171 935 7485; fax 0171 486 1349)

Menswear Womenswear, 207 Regent Street, London W1R 7DD (tel: 0171 439 6031)

Re-inforcements, 207 Regent Street, London W1R 7DD (tel: 0171 434 2644)

RHR (**Retail Human Resources** – wholesale, technical and design), 14 Bristol Gardens, Little Venice, London W9 2JG (tel: 0171 289 7622; fax 0171 289 1968)

Smith and Pye Fashion Recruitment, 26 Kingley Street, London W1R 5LB (tel: 0171 734 6200)

Star Executives, 9–10 Market Place, London W1N 7AH (tel: 0171 580 6725)

Success Design, 7 Air Street, London W1R 5RJ (tel: 0171 287 7722; fax 0171 734 1692)

Talisman Retail and Personnel Limited, Portland House, 4 Great Portland Street, London W1N 5AA (tel: 0171 307 1021)

Clearing houses for courses

Clearing House for Postgraduate Courses in Art and Design, Penn House, 9 Broad Street, Hereford HR4 9EP (tel: 01432 266653)

Graduate Teacher Training Registry, Fulton House, Jessop Avenue, Cheltenham, Gloucestershire GL50 3SH (tel: 01242 225868)

TEACH (**Teacher Education Admissions Clearing House**), PO Box 165, Holyrod Road, Edinburgh EH8 8AT (tel: 0131 558 6170)

UCAS (**Universities and Colleges Admissions Services**), PO Box 28, Cheltenham, Gloucestershire GL50 3SA (tel: 01242 222444 (application enquiries 01242 227788); Web site http:/www.ucas.ac.uk)

8 Further reading

General

Art World Directory, Arts Review – for gallery addresses

British Association of Art Therapists Limited – leaflets on art therapy

Butler, A (ed) *Making Ways – The visual artist's guide to surviving and thriving*, artist's newsletter

Careers in Conservation and Restoration, United Kingdom Institute for the Conservation of Historic and Artistic Works

Careers in Museums, Museums Association – available on request

Careers with an Arts Degree (1995), CRAC/Hobson

Chapman, N (1998) *Careers in Art and Design*, 8th edn, Kogan Page, London

Charlton, T (1985) *Guides to Courses and Careers in Art, Craft and Design*, National Society for Education in Art and Design

The Creative Handbook, Reed Information Services – a directory of design consultancies, illustrators, advertising agencies and so on

Department for Education and Employment publications – tel: 0845 602 2260; fax: 0845 603 3360; e-mail: dfee@prologcs. demon.co.uk

Edexel Foundation (Foundation for Educational Excellence) for various publications – Stewart House, 32 Russell Square, London WC1B 5DN (tel: 0171 393 4500; fax: 0171 393 4501)

Fine Art, Fashion and Textile Design, Two- and Three-dimensional Design, AGCAS – careers booklets

Golzen, G (1998) *Working for Yourself*, 18th edn, Kogan Page, London

London Art and Artists' Guide – galleries and sources of information

Museums and Galleries in Great Britain and Northern Ireland, Reed Information Services

Richardson, J (1998) *Careers in the Theatre*, 6th edn, Kogan Page, London

Running a Workshop: Basic business for craftspeople, Crafts Council

Selby, M (1997) *Careers in Television and Radio*, 7th edn, Kogan Page, London

Survive, Association of Illustrators

The Textile Institute – for various publications and course lists

Willings Press Guide, Reed Information Services – lists newspapers and periodicals

Writers' and Artists' Yearbook, A & C Black – published annually, this is a directory of newspapers, magazines and publishers, and has articles on finding an agency, copyright, self-marketing and so on

Course directories

A Guide to First Degree and Postgraduate Courses in Fashion Textile Design, The Association of Degree Courses in Fashion and Textile Design

The Degree Course Guide – Art and Design, Hobsons for CRAC – updated annually, this guide lists courses in art and design, and the history of craft and art

Design Courses, Trotman – updated annually, this is a starting point for those considering the study of a craft discipline, as the book describes courses from preparatory to postgraduate level, including teacher education

Guide to Courses in and Careers in Art, Crafts and Design, 6th edn, National Society for Education in Art and Design

Laser Compendium of Higher Education, Heinemann, Oxford

Mature Students Guide (1994), Trotman

The NATFHE Guide Handbook of Initial Teacher Training – for those considering a degree course in teaching

The Push Guide to Which University – also available on interactive CD ROM, it covers all courses and institutions

Scottish Universities' Entrance Guide, Scottish Universities' Council on Entrance

Stallard, M, *The Art and Design Directory*, AVEC Designs – updated annually, this directory gives details of first degree, HND and DipHE courses in art, design and communications

UCAS Handbook, UCAS

University Entrance Guide, UCAS – now handling clearing for art and design courses

Which Degree?, Newpoint Publishing

Grants

Grant booklets are available from your local education authority and from: Department for Education and Employment, Honeypot Lane, Canons Park, Stanmore, Middlesex HA7 1AZ; Scottish Education Department, Awards Branch, Gyleview House, 3 Redheughs Rigg, South Gyle, Edinburgh EH1 9HH; Department of Education for Northern Ireland, Ratgael House, Balloo Road, Bangor BT19 2PR, Northern Ireland

Guides to Grants – Postgraduate Awards, available from the Postgraduate Awards Division, HFE3, Honeypot Lane, Stanmore, Middlesex HA7 1AX

Student Grants and Loans — free booklet from the Department for Education and Employment

Additional information

Every area has a careers service with experts on hand to advise about careers. The careers advisers will also help you to make applications, put together your CV and write covering letters. If you are 18 or under, this help is free, though some offices extend this offer to people under 21. To contact your nearest careers service, look under 'Careers' in the telephone book.

The LWT programme *Wannabe* has a careers Web site at www.inn-tv.com.uk/wannabe or you can telephone 0171 757 7050 for a factsheet.

Journals and periodicals

Regular reading of the periodicals relevant to your interests is essential for keeping in touch with new developments, events, exhibitions, jobs and companies/consultancies/design groups you might want to work for.

The national press, such as *The Times*, the *Guardian* (creative and media appointments), *The Daily Telegraph*, *Daily Mail*, *The Sunday Times*, *The Observer*, *Sunday Telegraph* and *The Independent*, also advertise jobs in art and design, as do local newspapers from time to time. However, you may find that some of the specialist journals are the best, and sometimes only, places to start your search for a job or build your list of potential employers.

Key: W = weekly   M = monthly   Q = quarterly

A selection of these particularly useful to artists and designers is given below. See Chapter 7 for addresses. Items marked ★ are obtainable from newsagents.

Artist's Newsletter (M)
(AN Publications, PO Box 23,
Sunderland SR1 1BR)

job ads, bursaries, competitions, grants, news, reviews: for visual artists

*Association of Illustrators
Newsletter* (M)
(to members of AOI)

Campaign★

advertising, graphic design and other posts in design consultancies, publishing, arts, media, and market

Crafts (Bi-M)
(Crafts Council)

the magazine for the artist-craftsman; some vacancies, bursaries, workshop space

Current Vacancies (M) (from university careers services, or from the Central Services Unit, Crawford House, Precinct Centre, Oxford Road, Manchester M13 9EP)	posts generally open to graduates in all disciplines –
D Magazine (three times a year) (Gillard, Welch Limited, Chester Court, High Street, Knowle, Solihull B99 0LL)	
Design Week (W) (St Giles House, 50 Poland Street, London W1V 4AX)	design appointments
Draper's Record 'DR' (W)★	fashion and textile design, manufacture, retail/wholesale trade
Fashion Weekly (W)★	fashion design and production posts
Illustrator (Q) (magazine of the Association of Illustrators)	illustrators
Knitting Internation (M)★	knitwear design – some appointments in design and production
Museum Bulletin (M) (journal of the Museums Association)	all posts in national and provincial museums and art galleries; includes keepers, designers, conservators
The Stage and Television Today (W)★	posts in theatre
Time Out (W)★	arts, community projects, media – mostly in Greater London
The Times Educational Supplement (W)★ and *The Times Higher Education Supplement* (W)★	teaching posts in schools, colleges, higher education, remedial and art therapy

Fashion press and periodicals

The Clothes Show Magazine (M)
Elle (M)
The Face (M)
Harper's & Queen (M)
ID Magazine (M)
Marie Clarie (M)
19 (M)
Sky Magazine (Bi-M)
The Tatler (Ten times a year)
Vogue (M)
Dazed and Confused (M)

Fashion pages of the national press

The Guardian (Monday)
The Independent (Thursday and Sunday)
The Observer (Sunday)
The Times (Saturday and Sunday)
Weekend *Guardian* (Saturday)

Coventry University

Index

The Kogan Page *Careers in...* series

Careers in Accountancy *(6th edition)*

Careers in Architecture *(5th edition)*

Careers in Art and Design *(8th edition)*

Careers in Banking and Finance *(5th edition)*

Careers in Catering, Hotel Administration and Management *(5th edition)*

Careers in Computing and Information Technology

Careers in Environmental Conservation *(6th edition)*

Careers in Film and Video *(5th edition)*

Careers in Hairdressing and Beauty Therapy *(7th edition)*

Careers in Journalism *(8th edition)*

Careers in the Law *(8th edition)*

Careers in Marketing, Advertising and Public Relations *(6th edition)*

Careers in Medicine, Dentistry and Mental Health *(7th edition)*

Careers in Music

Careers in Nursing and Related Professions *(8th edition)*

Careers in the Police Service *(5th edition)*

Careers in Publishing and Bookselling *(2nd edition)*

Careers in Retailing *(6th edition)*

Careers in Secretarial and Office Work *(7th edition)*

Careers in Social Care *(7th edition)*

Careers in Sport *(7th edition)*

Careers in Teaching *(7th edition)*

Careers in Television and Radio *(7th edition)*

Careers in the Theatre *(6th edition)*

Careers in the Travel Industry *(6th edition)*

Careers Using English

Careers Using Languages *(8th edition)*

Careers Working with Animals *(8th edition)*

Careers in Working with Children and Young People *(7th edition)*

Careers Working Outdoors *(7th edition)*

Visit Kogan Page on-line

Comprehensive information on
Kogan Page titles

Features include

- complete catalogue listings,
  including book reviews and
  descriptions

- special monthly promotions

- information on NEW titles and
  BESTSELLING titles

- a secure shopping basket facility
  for on-line ordering